해커스
무역영어 1급
4주 완성 이론+기출문제

KB101079

실전 기출문제

해커스금융

\<제1과목\> 영문해석

[01 ~ 03] Read the following and answer.

Dear Ann,

Please quote for collection from our office and delivery to Busan port.

Our goods are:
- 6 divans and mattresses, 700㎝ × 480㎝
- 7 bookcase assembly kits packed in cardboard boxes, each measuring 14㎥
- 4 coffee-table assembly kits, packed in cardboard boxes.
- 4 armchairs, 320 × 190 × 260㎝

The divans and armchairs are fully protected against knocks and scratches by polythene and corrugated paper wrapping, and the invoiced value of the goods is USD 50,500. The freight will be borne by our customer.

I would appreciate a prompt reply, as delivery must be made before the end of next week.

01 What is the purpose of the letter above?
① request for a quotation of delivery
② request to deliver the goods by a deadline
③ offer of goods price being sold out
④ request for proper packing

02 Who is most likely to be Ann?
① buyer   ② seller
③ insurer   ④ freight forwarder

03 What Incoterms would be applied for the above transaction?
① FCA   ② CIP   ③ CFR   ④ FOB

04 Which is NOT suitable for the blank?

According to CISG, additional or different terms relating, among other things, to (   ) are considered to alter the terms of the offer materially.

① the price, payment, quality and quantity of the goods
② place and time of delivery
③ late acceptance
④ the settlement of disputes

[05 ~ 06] Read the following and answer the questions.

Dear Sirs,

We will be sending on behalf of our clients, Delta Computers, Ltd., a consignment of 20 computers to N.Z. Business Machines Pty., Wellington, New Zealand. The consignment is to be loaded on to the SS Northen Cross which sails from Tilbury on the 18th of May and is due in Wellington on the 25th of June.

We would be grateful if you could quote a rate covering all risks from port to port.

As the matter is urgent, we would appreciate a prompt reply.

Thank you.

Yours faithfully,

05 What is NOT included in the above?

① the subject-matter insured

② the name of vessel

③ the departing port and arriving port

④ insurable value

06 What is being sought?

① insurance premium

② freight

③ exchange rate

④ insurance amount

07 Below is a part of document. What is it?

> Whereas you have issued a bill of lading covering the above shipment and the above cargo has been arrived at the above port of discharge, we hereby request you to give delivery of the said cargo to the above mentioned party without production of the original bill of lading.
>
> In consideration of your complying with our above request, we hereby agree to indemnify you as follows:
>
> Expenses which you may sustain by reason of delivering the cargo in accordance with our request, provided that the undersigned Bank shall be exempt from liability for freight, demurrage or expenses in respect of the contract of carriage.
>
> As soon as the original bill of lading corresponding to the above cargo comes into our possession, we shall surrender the same to you, whereupon our liability hereunder shall cease.

① Shipping Letter of Guarantee

② Letter of Insurance

③ Delivery Guarantee

④ Demand Guarantee

08 According to the CISG, which one is regarded as a valid acceptance?

① Acceptance by silence

② Offerree's conduct indicating assent to the offer

③ Acceptance by inactivity

④ Counter offer for expiry extension

09 Which is NOT correct according to the following?

> Insurance policy in duplicate, endorsed in blank for 110% of the invoice cost. Insurance policy must include Institute Cargo Clauses ICC(B).

① Insurance certificate can be presented instead of insurance policy.

② In negotiating, blank endorsement must be made by a beneficiary.

③ 10% is added to the invoice cost as expected profit.

④ Insurance policy shall be issued in two original copies.

10 What is NOT proper contractual position according to CISG?

> We received your offer of April 1. 2018. After careful examination, we decided to accept your offer if you can reduce the price per set by US$2.

① The offeree reject the original offer.

② This terminates the offer.

③ This is a conditional acceptance.

④ This is a counter offer.

(A) Not only are we still waiting for part of our order to arrive, but once again we have received components (a) that should have sent to another department. We have forwarded them to the correct factory, and of course (b) we expect you to cover these costs. This is not the first time that this kind of mix-up has happened. (c) These delivery problems are causing us extra work as well as delays in production. We cannot accept this, and (d) will have to cancel the contract if it happens again.

11 Which of (a)~(d) is most grammatically INCORRECT?

① (a) ② (b) ③ (c) ④ (d)

12 What is the BEST sentence for blank (A)?

① I'm writing to amend our contract.

② I'm writing to complain about your latest delivery.

③ I'm writing to collect the money which you did not send.

④ I'm writing to inform you that I sent the components to the factory.

13 Who might be underlined 'you'?

We will shortly have a consignment of tape recorders, valued at £50,000 CIF Quebec, to be shipped from Manchester by a vessel of Manchester Liners Ltd.

We wish to cover the consignment against all risks from our warehouse at the above address to the port of Quebec. Will you please quote your rate for the cover.

① buyer ② carrier
③ insurance company ④ freight forwarder

14 Which is RIGHT statement according to UCP 600?

① In the absence of an indication to the contrary, the credit is deemed to be revocable.

② A revocable credit may be amended or cancelled only if all the basic parties of letter of credit agree with such amendment or cancellation.

③ A transferable credit can be transferred only no more than once.

④ An irrevocable credit may be amended or cancelled only by the issuing bank or the confirming bank.

15 Which of the following is not covered by Incoterms 2010?

① The parties are well advised to specify as clearly as possible the point within the named place of delivery.

② If the seller incurs costs under its contract of carriage related to unloading at the named place of destination, the seller is not entitled to recover such costs from the buyer unless otherwise agreed between the parties.

③ The seller is liable for any lack of conformity with the contract which is due to a breach of any of his obligations.

④ The buyer may provide the seller with appropriate evidence of having taken delivery.

16 Read the following and choose WRONG one in explaining Incoterms.

Different countries have different business cultures so it is a good idea to make sure we have a clear written contract to minimize the risk of misunderstandings. The contract should set out where the goods are being delivered. It should cover who is responsible for every stage of the journey, including customs clearance, and what insurance is required. It should also make it clear who pays for each different cost.

To avoid confusion, internationally agreed Incoterms should be used to spell out exactly what delivery terms are being agreed, such as:

① Where the goods will be delivered

② Who arranges transport

③ When the ownership of goods is transferred

④ Who handles customs procedures, and who pays any duties and taxes

17 Below is about contanerization. Which is NOT related to the practical container works?

> Containerization is a method of distributing the goods in a unitized form thereby allowing a multimodal transport system to be developed providing a possible combination of rail, road and ocean transport.
>
> As containers are becoming a very common method in multimodal transport, the course of business in container transport will be specified. Although not all containerized transport is multimodal, and vice versa, they are so often inter-related that it is useful to consider these two concepts together.

① Container transports are frequently arranged by freight forwarders.

② Containers are not necessarily owned by the carrier but often by companies specializing in containers which lend them to carriers.

③ If the exporter intends to stuff a full container load(FCL), shipping line may send an empty container to the exporter for loading.

④ If the cargo is less than a full container load(LCL), the exporter will send it to the container yard.

[18~19] Read the following and answer the questions

> Thank you for your inquiry regarding opening an account with our company. Please, fill in the enclosed financial information form and provide us with two or more trade references as well as one bank reference. Of course, all information will be kept in the strictest confidence.
>
> Thank you very much for your cooperation.

18 Which of the following is MOST likely to be found in the previous letter?

① We therefore request you to send us the names of three department stores with which your company already has accounts at present.

② If your company can supply us with two additional credit references as well as current financial statements, we will be pleased to reconsider your application.

③ We request that you open an account with us on 30-day credit terms, starting with the order listed.

④ I have enclosed our company's standard credit form for you to complete and would appreciate it if you would return it to me as soon as possible.

19 What would NOT be included in the underlined 'financial information'?

① balance sheet

② profit and loss account

③ cash flow

④ business registration certificate

20 Which is (are) suitable for the underlined 'rules'?

> When banks are asked to make payments as specified documents are presented to them, banks decide whether to pay or not based only upon the conformity or otherwise of the documents. The banks normally subscribe to an accepted set of definitions and <u>rules</u> of conduct and strict adherence to the rules is key to the efficient operation of banks' international trade finance.
>
> A. UCP 600 B. Incoterms 2010
> C. URC 522 D. ISP 98

① A only
② A + B only
③ A + C + D only
④ all of the above

21 Which of the following is NOT appropriate for the obligation of banks that are defined under URC 522?

① Banks will examine documents in order to obtain instructions.
② In the event that goods are dispatched directly to the address of a bank, such banks shall have no obligation to take delivery of the goods.
③ Banks will determine that the documents received appear to be as listed in the collection instruction.
④ Banks will act in good faith and exercise reasonable care.

22 Which of the following is right applicable law clause?

① Neither party shall be liable for failure to perform its part of this agreement when such failure is due to fire, flood, strikes, labour, troubles or other industrial disturbances, inevitable accidents, ware, embargoes, blockades, legal restrictions, riots, insurrections, or any cause beyond the control of the parties.

② All claims which can not be amicably settled between Sellers and Buyers shall be submitted to Arbitration in Seoul.
③ Unless specially stated, the trade terms under this contract shall be governed and construed under and by the latest Incoterms and the formation, validity, construction and the performance of this agreement are governed by CISG.
④ This agreement must be construed and take effect as a contract made in Korea, and the parties hereby submit to the jurisdiction of the court of Korea.

23 The following statement is a part of contract. What kind of clause is it?

> If any provision of this Agreement is subsequently held invalid or unenforceable by any court or authority agent, such invalidity or unenforceability shall in no way affect the validity of enforceability of any other provisions thereof.

① Non - waiver clause
② Infringement clause
③ Assignment clause
④ Severability clause

24 As defined by UCP 600, complying presentation means a presentation that is in accordance with :

> A. the terms and conditions of the credit
> B. the applicable provisions of UCP 600
> C. ISBP 745
> D. international standard banking practice

① A
② A + B
③ A + B + C
④ A + B + D

25 In accordance with UCP 600, what MUST the issuing bank do?

A documentary credit pre-advice is issued on 1 March for USD 500,000 with the following terms and conditions:
- Partial shipment allowed.
- Latest shipment date 30 April.
- Expiry date 15 May.

On 2 March the applicant requests an amendment prohibiting partial shipment and extending the expiry date to 30 May.

① Clarify with the applicant the period for presentation.
② Issue the documentary credit as originally instructed.
③ Issue the documentary credit incorporating all the amendments.
④ Issue the documentary credit incorporating only the extended expiry date.

<제2과목> 영작문

26 Who might be the underlined party?

Gentlemen,

As for the shipment of used furniture by S/S Arirang due to leave for Darkar in Senegal on the 21 May. Our partner, Socida Ltd, is to effect insurance on the goods as the contract is based on FOB.

They instructed us to effect a marine insurance contract with you on ICC(B) including War Risks at the rate which was mutually agreed upon by both of you.

① exporter
② importer
③ freight forwarder
④ underwriter

[27~28] Read the following and answer.

Dear Mr Kang,

With reference to your fax of 10 January 2018, we are pleased to inform you that we have identified a vessel that will meet your requirements.

She is the Arirang and is currently docked in Busan. She is a bulk carrier with a cargo (   ) of seven thousand tons. She has a maximum speed of 24 knots, so would certainly be capable of ten trips in the period you mentioned.

Please fax us to confirm the charter and we will send you the charter party.

27 Fill in the blank with suitable word.

① capacity   ② entrance
③ permission   ④ insurance

28 What type of transportation arrangement would best fit?

① voyage charter   ② time charter
③ speed charter   ④ bareboat charter

[29~31] Choose one which is NOT correctly composed into English.

29 ① 귀사의 서신에서 귀사가 면제품에 특별히 관심이 많다는 것을 알 수 있는데 이 분야에서는 당사가 전문가라 할 수 있습니다.
→ Your letter conveys us that you are specially interested in cotton goods, and we can say that we are specialists in this line.
② 당사는 25년 전에 설립된 전자제품 수출업체입니다.
→ Twenty five years have passed since we were established as an exporter of electronic goods.
③ 현재 시장상황이 불경기임에도 불구하고 만일 귀사가 경쟁력이 있다면 당사는 귀사와 거래를 시작할 수 있습니다.
→ Since at present the dullness rules the market, we are able to start a business with you unless you are in a competitive position.

④ 귀사가 다른 회사들처럼 가격을 10% 정도 할인해 주시거나 60일의 인수인도조건을 허용해 주시면 귀사의 청약을 수락하겠습니다.

→ If you would either discount the price by about 10% like other companies do or allow D/A at 60 days, we will accept your offer.

30 ① 계약이 체결되기 전까지 청약은 취소될 수 있습니다. 다만 이 경우에 취소의 통지는 피청약자가 승낙을 발송하기 전에 피청약자에게 도달하여야 합니다.

→ Until a contract is concluded, an offer may be revoked if the revocation reaches the offeree before an acceptance is dispatched by offeree.

② 매매계약은 서면에 의하여 체결되거나 또는 입증되어야 할 필요가 없으며, 또 형식에 관하여도 어떠한 다른 요건에 구속받지 아니합니다.

→ A contract of sales needs not be concluded in or evidenced by writing and is not subject to any other requirement as to form.

③ 보험서류에서 담보가 선적일보다 늦지 않은 일자로부터 유효하다고 보이지 않는 한 보험서류의 일자는 선적일보다 늦어서는 안됩니다.

→ The date of the insurance document must be no later than the date of shipment if it appears from the insurance document that the cover is effective until a date not later than the date of shipment.

④ 송하인의 지시식으로 작성되고 운임선지급 및 착하통지처가 발행의뢰인으로 표시된 무고장 선적해상선하증권의 전통을 제시하십시오.

→ Please submit full set of clean on board bill of lading made out to the order of shipper marked freight prepaid and notify applicant.

31 ① 동봉해 드린 주문서 양식에 정히 기입하셔서 즉시 반송해 주시길 바랍니다.

→ We suggest that you return to us straightway the enclosed order form duly filled in.

② 주문이 쇄도해서 귀사가 주문한 미니 컴퓨터는 매진 되었습니다.

→ The mini-computers you ordered are sold out owing to the rush of orders.

③ 면셔츠 가격이 상당히 치솟았으나 종전 가격으로 귀사 주문품을 조달해 드리겠습니다.

→ The prices of cotton shirts have soared considerably, but we can fill your order at the former prices.

④ 이번 구매로 상당한 이익이 될 것이며 더 많은 주문을 하게 될 것으로 믿습니다.

→ We believe this purchase will bring you a good profit and result from your further orders.

32 What is the correct wordings for the consignee column of the B/L under the following L/C requirement?

> A Credit, which was issued by American Commercial Bank, requires a document that "full set of clean on board ocean bills of lading made out to our order and notify applicant".

① To order of American Commercial Bank
② To order of Shipper
③ To order
④ To order of applicant

[33~34] Read the following and answer the questions

> I regret to inform you that an error was made on our invoice number B 832 of 18 August. 100 pieces of polyester shirts were sent.
> The correct charge for polyester shirts, medium, is £26.70 per piece and not £26.00 as stated. We are therefore enclosing a (ⓐ) for the amount undercharged, namely £(ⓑ).
> This mistake was due to an input error and we are sorry it was not noticed before the invoice was sent

33 Fill in the blanks with the most suitable answer.

① ⓐ charge – ⓑ 26.70
② ⓐ debit note – ⓑ 70.0
③ ⓐ payment – ⓑ 26.0
④ ⓐ credit note – ⓑ 267.0

34 Who is the sender of the letter?

① buyer   ② banker

③ supplier   ④ shipping agent

[35~36] Read the following and answer the questions.

> Dear Mr. Sheridan,
>
> We are currently planning to add yard and garden tractors to our line of leased equipment. It is my pleasure to announce that we shall feature your line of Titan tractors.
>
> Would you please send us a catalog containing a complete list of models, specifications, and price terms for Titan tractors. In particular, we require data in attached file on each model.
>
> We need <u>this information</u> no later than September 30 in order to include it in our November catalog.
>
> We are delighted to have found such an excellent line of products, and we look forward to a pleasant and profitable business relationship.

35 Which is LEAST likely to be included in the underlined 'this information'?

① sales terms

② credit reference

③ product lines

④ product specifications

36 Who is Mr. Sheridan MOST likely to be?

① sales manager

② credit manager

③ personnel manager

④ accountant

37 Fill in the blank with suitable word(s).

> Trade finance generally refers to the financing of individual transactions or a series of revolving transactions. And, trade finance loans are often (   ), that is, the lending bank stipulates that all sales proceeds are to be collected, and then applied to payoff the loan. The remainder is credited to the exporter's account.

① self liquidating   ② repaid later

③ added separately   ④ easily taken

38 Below explains voyage charter. Fill in the blank with right word.

> A voyage charter is the hiring of a vessel and crew for a voyage between a load port and a discharge port. The charterer pays the vessel owner on a per ton or lump-sum basis. The owner pays the port costs, fuel costs and crew costs. The payment for the use of the vessel is known as freight. A voyage charter specifies a period, known as (   ), for loading and unloading the cargo.

① tenor   ② transit time

③ off hire   ④ laytime

39 Below is about marine insurance. Fill in the blank with right word(s).

> While cargo is usually insured against the perils of the sea, which are defined as natural accidents peculiar to the sea, most ship owners carry hull insurance on their ships and protect themselves against claims by third parties by purchasing (   ) insurance.

① protection and indemnity

② vessel

③ Institute Cargo Clauses

④ open policy

40 What could best replace the underlined words?

Forfaiting involves the purchase of trade receivables without recourse, meaning that the purchasing bank or finance company cannot claim against the original ⓐ trade creditor in the event that the ⓑ trade debtor refuses or is unable to pay its obligations when due. A frequent exception is when non-payment is due to a trade dispute between the seller and buyer, who claims the seller did not ship the right goods or otherwise committed fraud in the transaction.

① ⓐ seller – ⓑ buyer
② ⓐ bank – ⓑ seller
③ ⓐ insurer – ⓑ buyer
④ ⓐ buyer – ⓑ insurer

41 Below explains some characteristics of insurance. Make a suitable pair for (ⓐ) and (ⓑ).

Some policies include either an (ⓐ) or (ⓑ) clause. (ⓐ) represents a predetermined amount that is deducted from a claim and is used to discourage irresponsible, malicious and small claims. (ⓑ) means a percentage of the value of a loss, below which no payment is made but above which total compensation is paid.

① ⓐ Excess – ⓑ Franchise
② ⓐ Franchise – ⓑ Excess
③ ⓐ minimum – ⓑ maximum
④ ⓐ maximum – ⓑ minimum

42 This is a letter advising the issuance of L/C. Which is a right match?

Gentlemen :
ⓐ We have arranged with ⓑ the Bank of America for an Irrevocable Letter of Credit in your favor for US.$125,000. ⓒ Korea Exchange Bank, in your city, will send you the L/C which ⓓ you will receive within a few days.

① ⓐ We – beneficiary
② ⓐ the Bank of America – reimbursing bank
③ ⓐ Korea Exchange Bank – advising bank
④ ⓐ you – applicant

43 What is MOST suitable for the blank below?

Payment can be deferred in the case of a/an ( ) which gives time for the buyer to inspect or even sell the goods.

① restricted L/C   ② usance L/C
③ straight L/C   ④ revocable L/C

44 Choose the most appropriate set of words to complete the sentences.

For carriers, (ⓐ) simply means the seller/shipper is responsible for stuffing the container and the cost thereof. The shipping line receives the containers at (ⓑ) and does not commit itself as regards the contents.
On the other hand, (ⓒ) means that the carrier is responsible for the suitability and condition of the container, and the stuffing thereof. The containers are filled or stuffed on the carrier's premises, ideally at a (ⓓ). Therefore, it has become accepted practice combining (ⓔ) with (ⓕ), and (ⓖ) with (ⓗ).

	ⓐ	ⓑ	ⓒ	ⓓ	ⓔ	ⓕ	ⓖ	ⓗ
①	LCL	CY	FCL	CFS	LCL	CY	FCL	CFS
②	LCL	CFS	FCL	CY	LCL	CFS	FCL	CY
③	FCL	CY	LCL	CFS	FCL	CY	LCL	CFS
④	FCL	CFS	LCL	CY	FCL	CFS	LCL	CY

45 Choose the most appropriate set of words to complete the sentences.

> A bill of lading is a ( ) instrument and can be passed from a shipper through any number of parties, each party ( ) it to assign title to the next party. The only condition is that ( ) can be assigned only by the party shown on the bill as having ( ) at the time. Any failure to respect this condition breaks what is known as the chain of title; all purported assignments of title after such a break are invalid.

① negotiable – endorsing – title – title
② transferable – naming – delivery – delivery
③ transferable – endorsing – delivery – delivery
④ negotiable – naming – title – delivery

46 Choose the WRONG one which explains EXW in respect of loading.

① The seller has no obligation to the buyer to load the goods, even though in practice the seller may be in a better position to do so.
② If the seller does load the goods, it does so at the buyer's risk and expense.
③ In cases where the seller is in a better position to load the goods, FCA is usually more appropriate.
④ EXW obliges the seller to load at its own risk and expense.

47 What does the following refer to?

> Any extraordinary sacrifice or expenditure is voluntarily and reasonably made or incurred in time of peril for the purpose of preserving the property imperilled in the common adventure.

① total loss
② particular average
③ general average
④ partial loss

[48 ~ 49] Read the following and answer.

> The most common transfer document is the bill of lading. The bill of lading is a (ⓐ) given by the freight company to the shipper. A bill of lading serves as a document of title and specifies who is to receive the merchandise at designated port. It can be in non-negotiable or in negotiable form. In a ⓑ straight bill of lading, the seller consigns the goods directly to the buyer. This type of bill is usually not desirable in a letter of credit transaction, because it allows the buyer to obtain possession of the merchandise without regard to any bank agreement for repayment.

48 Fill in the blank (ⓐ) with right word.
① receipt   ② evidence
③ proof   ④ exchange

49 What is best substitute for 'ⓑ straight'?
① order   ② usance
③ sight   ④ special

50 Fill in the blank with suitable words.

> If a contract is silent on the country of the proper court, the parties involved in a dispute may want to invoke the jurisdiction of the national courts in which they think they have the highest likelihood of success, or the courts which are most convenient for them. This practice is known as ( ).

① forum seeking
② forum shopping
③ court tour
④ court reference

<제3과목> 무역실무

51 ( ) 안에 들어갈 용어를 올바르게 나열한 것은?

> (a)는 선박의 밀폐된 내부 전체용적을 나타내며 100ft³을 1톤으로 하되 기관실, 조타실 따위의 일부 시설물의 용적은 제외한다. 각국의 보유 선복량 표시, 관세, 등록세, 도선료 등의 부과 기준이 된다. 반면 (b)는 상행위에 직접적으로 사용되는 장소만을 계산한 용적으로 전체 내부용적에서 선원실, 갑판창고, 통신실, 기관실 따위를 제외한 부분을 톤수로 환산한 것이며, 톤세, 항세, 항만시설사용료, 운하통과료 등의 부과 기준이 된다.

① a : 총톤수(G/T : gross tonnage)
   b : 순톤수(N/T : net tonnage)
② a : 순톤수(N/T : net tonnage)
   b : 총톤수(G/T : gross tonnage)
③ a : 재화중량톤수(DWT : dead weight ton)
   b : 배수톤수(displacement ton)
④ a : 배수톤수(displacement ton)
   b : 재화중량톤수(DWT : dead weight ton)

52 Incoterms 2010상 FCA 조건에 대한 설명이다. ( ) 안에 들어갈 내용을 올바르게 나열한 것은?

> 물품의 지정된 인도장소가 매도인의 영업장 구내인 경우에는, (a)이 매수인 지정 운송수단에 적재책임을 부담한다. 그리고 기타의 경우에는, 물품이 매도인의 (b) 상태로 매수인이 지정한 운송인이나 제3자의 임의처분 하에 놓인 때이다.

① a : 매도인, b : 운송수단에 실린 채 양륙 준비된
② a : 매수인, b : 운송수단으로부터 양륙 완료된
③ a : 매수인, b : 운송수단에 실린 채 양륙 준비된
④ a : 매도인, b : 운송수단으로부터 양륙 완료된

53 산업설비수출계약이나 해외건설공사계약을 체결한 수출자가 계약상의 의무이행을 하지 않음으로써 발주자가 입게 되는 손해를 보상받기 위해 발행하는 수출보증서로 옳은 것은?

① Retention Bond
② Performance Bond
③ Maintenance Bond
④ Advanced Payment Bond

54 무역계약의 성립요건에 대한 설명으로 옳지 않은 것은?

① 계약의 목적과 내용이 위법이거나 실현 불가능한 것이어서는 안 된다.
② 계약당사자의 행위능력이 있어야 한다.
③ 사기나 강박 등에 의한 것이 아니어야 한다.
④ 착오에 의한 계약도 유효하므로 계약체결 시 유의하여야 한다.

55 Incoterms 2010상 복합운송조건에 대한 설명으로 옳지 않은 것은?

① 해상운송이 전혀 포함되지 않은 경우에도 사용 가능하다.
② 해상운송만 이용되는 경우에도 문제없이 사용할 수 있다.
③ 선택된 운송방식이 어떤 것인지, 운송방식이 단일운송인지 복합운송인지 불문하고 사용가능하다.
④ 복합운송 중 최초의 운송방식이 해상운송인 경우에도 사용가능하다.

56 신용장통일규칙(UCP 600)에서 규정하고 있는 선하증권의 수리요건으로 볼 수 없는 것은?

① 운송인의 명칭과 운송인, 선장 또는 지정 대리인이 서명한 것
② 신용장에 지정된 선적항과 양륙항을 명시한 것
③ 화물의 본선적재가 인쇄된 문언으로 명시되어 있거나 본선 적재필이 부기된 것
④ 용선계약에 따른다는 명시가 있을 것

57 환어음을 작성할 필요가 없는 결제방법은?

① Freely Negotiable Credit

② D/P

③ D/A

④ COD

58 신용장방식의 경우 곡물, 광산물과 같은 bulk cargo의 선적수량에 대한 설명으로 옳은 것은?

① 일반적으로 3%의 과부족을 용인한다.

② 일반적으로 5%의 과부족을 용인한다.

③ 일반적으로 10%의 과부족을 용인한다.

④ 일체의 과부족을 용인하지 않는다.

59 수출상과 수입상이 동종의 물품을 일정기간에 걸쳐 반복적으로 거래할 경우 한번 개설된 신용장의 효력이 일정기간 경과 후 다시 갱생되는 신용장은?

① 선대신용장   ② 회전신용장

③ 기탁신용장   ④ 토마스신용장

60 국제물품매매계약에 관한 UN협약(CISG)에서 매도인이 계약을 위반했을 때 매수인에게 부여할 권리구제의 방법에 대한 설명으로 옳지 않은 것은?

① 매도인이 계약을 이행하지 않는 경우에 매수인은 원칙적으로 계약대로의 이행을 청구할 수 있다.

② 매수인은 매도인의 의무이행을 위하여 합리적인 추가기간을 지정할 수 있다.

③ 매수인이 수령당시와 동등한 상태로 반환할 수 없는 경우에도 대체물품인도청구권을 가질 수 있다.

④ 매도인이 물품의 하자를 보완하였거나 매수인이 매도인의 보완제의를 부당하게 거절하는 경우 대금감액은 인정되지 않는다.

61 Incoterms 2010상 DAP와 DAT 조건에 대한 설명이다. ( ) 안에 들어갈 내용을 올바르게 나열한 것은?

> DAP와 DAT는 모두 도착지인도 규칙(delivered rule)으로서, (a) 사용될 수 있다. DAP와 DAT는 인도(delivery)가 지정목적지(named place of destination)에서 일어난다는 공통점이 있으나, 구체적으로 (b)에서는 물품이 그러한 목적지에서 운송수단으로부터 양륙된 상태로 매수인의 처분 하에 놓인 때에, (c)에서는 물품이 그러한 도착지에서 운송수단에 실린 채 양륙 준비된 상태로 매수인의 임의처분 하에 놓인 때에 인도가 일어난다는 차이가 있다.

① a : 운송방식에 관계없이, b : DAT, c : DAP

② a : 해상운송 및 내수로 운송에, b : DAT, c : DAP

③ a : 운송방식에 관계없이, b : DAP, c : DAT

④ a : 해상운송 및 내수로 운송에, b : DAP, c : DAT

62 청약의 소멸사유로 옳지 않은 것은?

① 청약에 대한 상대방의 승낙

② 청약의 철회(withdrawal)

③ 당사자의 사망

④ 청약의 거절 또는 반대청약

63 신용장에서 "Manually Signed Commercial Invoice in triplicate certifying goods as per 'Description of Goods' and to be of CHINESE origin. Original Invoice to be legalized by UAE Embassy/Consulate" 라고 기재된 경우, 옳지 않은 것은?

① 송장상에 서명은 반드시 수기로 하여야 한다.

② 송장 3부 모두 반드시 원본으로 제시하여야 한다.

③ 송장상에 물품의 원산지가 중국임을 증명하는 내용이 포함되어 있어야 한다.

④ 송장 원본은 반드시 아랍에미레이트 대사관에서 직인(확인)을 받아야 한다.

64 해상운임에 대한 설명으로 옳지 않은 것은?

① 귀금속 등 고가의 운송에 있어 화물의 가격을 기초로 일정률을 징수하는 종가운임이 있다.

② 화물의 용적이나 중량이 일정기준 이하일 경우 최저 운임이 적용된다.

③ 중량 또는 용적 중 운임이 높은 쪽으로 실제운임을 부과하는 중량톤(revenue ton)이 있다.

④ 화물, 장소, 화주에 따라 운임을 차별적으로 부과하는지의 여부에 따라 차별운임과 무차별운임이 있다.

65 공동해손비용손해(general average expenditure)에 해당하지 않는 것은?

① 인양비용
② 피난항 비용
③ 임시 수리비
④ 손해방지비용

66 Incoterms 2010상 EXW(Ex Works) 조건에 대한 설명으로 옳지 않은 것은?

① 매도인은 매매계약과 일치하는 물품을 자신의 영업장 구내에서 매수인에게 인도한다.

② 당사자 사이에 합의되었거나 관습이 있는 경우에 서류는 그에 상당하는 전자적 기록이나 절차로 할 수 있다.

③ 매수인은 매도인의 영업장 구내에서 물품을 수령하고 이를 입증하는 적절한 증빙을 제공하여야 한다.

④ 매도인은 수출국에 의하여 강제적인 검사를 포함하여 모든 선적 전 검사 비용을 부담하여야 한다.

67 혼재 서비스(Consolidation Service)에 대한 설명으로 옳지 않은 것은?

① 공동혼재(Joint Consolidation)는 운송주선인이 자체적으로 집화한 소량화물을 FCL로 단위화하기에 부족한 경우 동일 목적지의 LCL을 확보하고 있는 타 운송주선인과 FCL 화물을 만들기 위해 업무를 협조하는 것이다.

② Buyer's Consolidation은 운송주선인이 한 사람의 수입상으로부터 위탁을 받아 다수의 수출상으로부터 화물을 집화하여 컨테이너에 혼재한 후 그대로 수입상에게 운송하는 형태이다. CFS‒CY 형태로 운송된다.

③ Forwarder's Consolidation은 운송주선인이 여러 화주의 소량 컨테이너화물을 CFS에서 혼재한다. 혼재된 화물은 목적항의 CFS에서 화주별로 분류되어 해당 수입상에게 인도된다. CY‒CY 형태로 운송된다.

④ Shipper's Consolidation은 수출상이 여러 수입상에게 송부될 화물을 혼재하는 것이다. CY‒CFS 형태로 운송된다.

68 중재(Arbitration)에 의한 분쟁의 해결에 대한 설명으로 옳지 않은 것은?

① 중재합의의 주요 내용으로 중재지, 중재기관, 준거법을 포함해야 한다.

② 중재합의는 반드시 서면으로 이뤄져야 한다.

③ 중재절차의 심문은 비공개를 원칙으로 서면주의와 구술주의를 병행한다.

④ 중재절차에서 당사자 일방이 심문에 출석하지 아니하면 심문절차는 진행되지 않는다.

69 원산지증명서에 대한 설명으로 옳지 않은 것은?

① 원산지증명서는 양허세율의 적용 시 기준으로 이용되기도 한다.

② 일반적인 원산지증명서는 대한상공회의소에서 발급하고 있다.

③ 관세양허 원산지증명서는 세관에서도 발급하고 있다.

④ 원산지증명서에서 수화인의 정보는 운송서류상의 수화인의 정보와 다르게 표시할 수 있다.

70 서류의 용도가 다른 하나는?

① Letter of Guarantee

② Letter of Indemnity

③ Surrendered B/L

④ Sea Waybill

71 무역금융 융자대상이 되지 않는 것은?

① D/A, D/P 방식에 의한 물품 수출

② 중계무역방식에 의한 물품 수출

③ CAD, COD 방식에 의한 물품 수출

④ 구매확인서에 의한 수출용 원자재의 국내 공급

72 다음의 경우 환가료를 원화로 계산한 것으로 옳은 것은?

| 1) 거래금액 : USD 8,000 |
| 2) 거래조건 : A/S |
| 3) 환가료율 : 2.00% |
| 4) 우편일수 : 9일 |
| 5) 환율(장부가격) : USD 1 = KRW 1,100 |

① 1,600원

② 4,400원

③ 16,000원

④ 44,000원

73 신용장통일규칙(UCP 600)상 '신용장양도'에 관한 설명으로 옳지 않은 것은?

① 신용장이 양도가능하기 위해서는 신용장에 "양도가능(transferable)"이라고 기재되어야 한다.

② 양도은행이라 함은 신용장을 양도하는 지정은행을 말하며, 개설은행은 양도은행이 될 수 없다.

③ 양도와 관련하여 발생한 모든 수수료는 제1수익자가 부담하는 것이 원칙이다.

④ 제2수익자에 의한 또는 그를 대리하여 이루어지는 서류의 제시는 양도은행에 이루어져야 한다.

74 운송계약의 당사자인 운송인은 용선자가 아니라 선주 또는 선박임차인이고, 선하증권의 효력이 선하증권 소지인과 선주 간에만 미치므로 운송 중 화물의 손해에 대해 용선자는 아무런 책임도 부담하지 않는다는 취지의 조항은?

① Jason Clause

② Himalaya Clause

③ Demise Clause

④ Indemnity Clause

75 수출자 또는 수출 물품 등의 제조업자에 대한 외화획득용 원료 또는 물품 등의 공급 중 수출에 공하여 지는 것으로 수출실적의 인정범위에 해당하지 않는 것은?

① 내국신용장(Local L/C)에 의한 공급

② 내국신용장(Local L/C)의 양도에 의한 공급

③ 구매확인서에 의한 공급

④ 산업통상자원부장관이 지정하는 생산자의 수출 물품 포장용 골판지상자의 공급

<제1과목> 영문해석

01 What is WRONG in Incoterms 2010 explanation?

① CIF : Seller is not responsible for the condition of the goods while they are in pre - carriage transit.

② CIF : Same as CFR, except for the insurance coverage.

③ CPT : Direct extension of the FCA Incoterm. It switches the contract of main - carriage task from the buyer to the seller.

④ CPT : Seller is not responsible for the condition of the goods during vessel loading when the loading takes place after the goods have been delivered to the previous carrier.

02 Which has a different topic from others?

① We are pleased to say that we can deliver the goods by November 1, so you will have stock for the Christmas sales period.

② As there are regular sailings from Busan to New York, we are sure that the goods will reach you well within the time you specified.

③ We have the materials in stock and will ship them immediately on receipt of your order.

④ All list prices are quoted FOB Busan and are subject to a 25% trade discount with payment by letter of credit.

[03 ~ 04] Read the following and answer.

Dear Mr Han,

We are pleased to tell you that the above order has been shipped on the SS Marconissa and should reach you in the next 30 days. Meanwhile, our bank has forwarded the <u>relevant documents</u> and draft for USD 3,000,000 which includes the agreed trade and quantity discounts, to HSBC Seoul for your acceptance of the draft.

We are sure you will be very satisfied with the consignment and look forward to your next order.

Best wishes,

William Cox
Daffodil Computer

03 What payment method can be inferred?

① COD　　② CAD　　③ D/P　　④ D/A

04 Which document is most far from the underlined 'relevant documents'?

① bill of exchange

② commercial invoice

③ packing list

④ bill of lading

05 Which is most far from usage of export credit insurance?

① It protects against financial cost of non - payment by buyer.

② It enables exporters to offer buyers competitive payment terms.

③ It helps to obtain working capital loans from banks.

④ It protects against losses from damage of goods in transit.

06 Who might be A?

Transport documents are required both to assure that the goods are being properly transported and for the A to claim possession of the goods at destination.

① buyer   ② seller

③ carrier   ④ banks

07 Which is MOST suitable for (A)?

A credit requiring an "invoice" without further definition will be satisfied by any type of invoice presented except : (A)

① customs invoice

② tax invoice

③ consular invoice

④ pro-forma invoice

08 Which is correct according to CISG?

On 1 July Seller delivered an offer, which is valid until 30 Sep 2018, to Buyer. On 15 July Buyer sent letter "I do not accept your offer because the price is too high" but on 10 August the Buyer sent again "I hereby accept your prior offer of 1 July". Seller immediately responded that he could not treat this "acceptance" because of Buyer's earlier rejection.

① Buyer can not insist his last acceptance.

② Seller shall accommodate the buyer's acceptance.

③ As long as the offer is valid, buyer can claim his last acceptance.

④ Buyer is able to withdraw his first acceptance.

09 Choose one which describes BEST for (a) ~ (d).

(a) We have drawn a draft at sight for US$35,000 on (b) the Bank of New York, N.Y. under the L/C No. 089925 and negotiated it through (c) the Korea Exchange Bank, Seoul, Korea.

Please note that all documents required in the Letter of Credit were forwarded to our (d) negotiating bank as per copies attached.

① (a) is an applicant of the Credit.

② (b) is a drawee of the Bill of Exchange.

③ (c) is a drawer of the Bill of Exchange.

④ (d) is Bank of New York.

10 In the following situation, which BEST suits the exporter's needs?

An exporter is willing to release the shipping documents directly to the buyer, but wishes to retain some guarantee of payment should the buyer fail to pay on the due date.

① Red Clause L/C   ② Transferable L/C

③ Confirmed L/C   ④ Standby L/C

11 What is the maximum value available for this final drawing?

A beneficiary receives an irrevocable documentary credit for which USD 20,000 may be drawn during each month of the documentary credit's one year validity. The documentary credit also indicates that reinstatement is on a cumulative basis. Full monthly drawings were made during the first, second, fourth, fifth and seventh months and there have been no other drawings. In the last month of the documentary Credit's validity, the beneficiary expects to make a final shipment.

① USD 80,000   ② USD 100,000

③ USD 120,000   ④ USD 140,000

12 What kind of contract is the below?

> Bailment of goods to another (bailee) for sale under agreement that bailee will pay bailor for any sold goods and will return any unsold goods.

① contract of sale
② offer on approval
③ sole agent agreement
④ consignment contract

13 Below is a reply to a letter. Which of the following is the MOST appropriate title for the previous letter?

> Thank you for your interest in our solutions at Bespoke Solutions Inc. We are a leading software development firm with an impressive track record creating responsive solutions to support organizational objectives. We offer a broad range of website development solutions. Attached is our comprehensive price list, please find.

① Request for Acceptance
② Request for Quotation(RFQ)
③ Purchase Order(P/O)
④ Shipment Notice

[14~15] Read the following and answer the questions.

> Dear Chapman,
> We were pleased to receive your order of 15th April for a further supply of transistor sets, but as the balance of your account now stands at over USD400,000, we hope you will be able to reduce it before we grant credit for further supplies.
> We should therefore be grateful if you could send us your check for, say, half the amount you owe us. We could then arrange to supply the goods you now ask for and <u>charge</u> them to your account.
> Yours faithfully,
> Brown Kim

14 Which is MOST similar to the underlined 'charge'?

① remove ② allow   ③ credit   ④ debit

15 Which is LEAST correct about the letter?

① Chapman placed an order with Brown.
② The writer is reluctant to extend credit.
③ The action of this letter resulted from the previous account which remains unpaid.
④ Brown Kim wants the overdue to be reduced at least by USD 200,000 this time.

16 Which of the following is grammatically INCORRECT?

> (a) <u>I am afraid I have noticed</u> there is a word missing (b) <u>in the final version of our contract.</u> (c) <u>I would like you to take a look at i</u>t and determine (d) <u>whether it is enough big to cause a dispute.</u> Once again, I give you my sincerest apologies for the inconvenience.

① (a)   ② (b)   ③ (c)   ④ (d)

[17~18] Read the following and answer the questions.

> Dear Mr. Edwards,
> Thank you for letting us know about the roses that arrived at your company in less perfect condition. I enclose a check refunding your full purchase price.
> An unexpected delay in the repair of our loaded delivery van, coupled with an unusual rise in temperatures last Thursday, caused the deterioration of your roses. Please accept our apology and our assurance that steps will be taken to prevent this from happening again.
> During the past fifteen years, it has been our pleasure to number you among our valued customers, whose satisfaction is the goal we are

constantly striving to achieve. I sincerely hope you will continue to count on us for your needs.

Yours very truly,

Thomas Sagarino

17 Which is LEAST correct about the letter?

① Mr. Edwards is a longtime customer.

② Thomas believes that Edwards has a legitimate complaint.

③ Mr. Edwards asked for an exchange because some of the roses were missing.

④ Thomas Sagarino is a supplier.

18 What is the main purpose of the letter?

① Goodwill with the customers

② Confirming the order

③ Apology for damaged goods

④ Appreciation for the business

19 Which is most WRONG about the difference between EXW and FCA under Incoterms 2010?

① In terms of EXW, the obligation of delivery of goods by the seller is only limited to arrange goods at his premises.

② In terms of FCA, the export cleared goods are delivered by the seller to the carrier at the named and defined location mentioned in the contract.

③ In terms of FCA, the delivery of goods also can be at the seller's premises, if mutually agreed between buyer and seller.

④ If the buyer can not carry out the export formalities, either directly or indirectly, EXW terms are opted in such business transactions.

[20~21] Read the following and answer the questions.

We have received your letter of 23rd May enclosing your Debit Note No. 123. We are sorry not to have paid your account earlier by (a).

In payment of these accounts, we enclose a check for USD 5,000,000 (b) <u>covering your invoice up to the end of May 2018</u>.

We shall be obliged if you will send us a receipt by return of post.

20 Which of the following is MOST appropriate for (a)?

① an oversight   ② a request

③ a credit   ④ an order

21 What is the MOST accurate Korean translation on (b)?

① 2018년 5월말까지 보내올 송장을 해결하기 위하여

② 2018년 5월말까지 귀사의 송장 대금을 결제하는

③ 2018년 5월말에 보낼 귀사의 송장에 포함시키기 위하여

④ 2018년 5월말에 보내 주신 송장을 처리하기 위하여

22 Which of the following is the MOST appropriate purpose of the letter below?

Dear Alice,

Thank you for your call this afternoon and your interest in my business development services. It was great talking to you and discussing your business concept and expansion plans for Alize Catering.

As discussed during our telephone conversation :

You would like me to develop a detailed business plan for Alize Catering.

The business plan will set out guidelines for Alize Catering operations in terms of the:

Organizational plan, Production plan, Marketing Plan, and Financial plan.

> The total cost for the development of the business plan is USD 3,000 payable in 3 installments, with the first installment due immediately as confirmation of this engagement, the 2nd due on receipt of the draft document, and the 3rd due on delivery of the final document.

① To confirm a verbal agreement
② To inform about a new product
③ To request free product samples
④ To cancel the order

23 Which is a LEAST appropriate match?

> A (a) <u>forwarder</u> booked $2 \times 20'$ containers with (b) <u>a shipping line</u> to Doha on behalf of (c) <u>his client</u>.
> Due to a mistake of the shipping line staff, the shipping line shipped $1 \times 20'$ to Doha and put the other $1 \times 20'$ with some other clients' container and shipped it to Bremerhaven. By the time the forwarder found this mistake out, the container was already on its way to (d) <u>Bremerhaven</u>. The shipping line has advised that this container will be rerouted but the container will take about 60 days to reach Doha instead of the original transit time of 20 days if it had gone directly.

① (a) is a NVOCC
② (b) is a VOCC
③ (c) is an exporter
④ (d) is an original destination

24 Which of the following has a different intention from others?

① They deserve your confidence and credit in the sum you mentioned.
② The company enjoys an excellent reputation among the business circles here.
③ You may run the least risk in granting the said credit in this deal.
④ After three months' experience of delay, we were obliged to withdraw credit privileges from them.

25 What is LEAST likely to be the one which the seller writes?

① A batten-reinforced case would meet your needs and be much lower in price than a solid wooden case.
② The 1lb. size cans of chemicals will be shipped in strong cartons, each containing 24 cans.
③ When all items of the order are collected at our factory, we will pack them into suitable sizes for delivery.
④ Overall measurements of each case must not exceed 80cm(L) × 50cm(W) × 40cm(D).

<제2과목> 영작문

[26~28] Read the following and answer.

A sight draft is used when the exporter wishes to retain title to the shipment until it reaches its destination and payment is made.

In actual practice, the ocean bill of lading is endorsed by the exporter and sent via the exporter's bank to the buyer's bank. It is accompanied by the sight draft, invoices, and other supporting documents that are specified by either the buyer or the buyer's country. The foreign bank notifies the buyer when it has received these documents. As soon as the draft is paid, the (A) foreign bank turns over the bill of lading thereby enabling the buyer to obtain the shipment.

There is still some risk when a sight draft is used to control transferring the title of a shipment. The buyer's ability or willingness to pay might change from the time the goods are shipped until the time the drafts are presented for payment ; (B)

26 What is suitable payment method for the above transaction?

① D/P   ② D/A
③ Sight L/C   ④ Usance L/C

27 Who is (A)?

① collecting bank   ② remitting bank
③ issuing bank   ④ nego bank

28 What is a most proper sentence for blank (B)?

① there is no bank promise to pay on behalf of the buyer.
② the presenting bank is liable for the buyer's payment.
③ the seller shall ask the presenting bank to ship back the goods.
④ the carrier asks the buyer to provide indemnity for release of the goods.

29 Which is NOT proper replacement for the underlined?

Dear team,
Our company is facing <u>regular</u> shipments to East Asian countries so that we will need to review cost scheme in relation to transportation and insurance.
Please note that meeting will be held on next week Monday 9:00 A.M. in my office.
Tony Han
General Manager

① customary
② usual
③ normal
④ punctual

30 Which of the following statements on INCOTERMS 2010 is NOT correct?

ⓐ The Incoterms 2010 rules are standard shipment term designed to assist traders when goods are sold and transported. ⓑ Each Incoterms rule specifies the obligations of each party(e.g. who is responsible for services such as transport; import and export clearance etc), and ⓒ the point in the journey where risk transfers from the seller to the buyer. ⓓ By agreeing on an Incoterms rule and incorporating it into the sales contract, the buyer and seller can achieve a precise understanding of what each party is obliged to do, and where responsibility lies in event of loss, damage or other mishap.

① ⓐ   ② ⓑ   ③ ⓒ   ④ ⓓ

[31 ~ 32] Read the following and answer.

Dear Mr. Cho,

Your name was given to us (A) Mr. L. Crane, the chief buyer of F. Lynch & Co. Ltd, who have asked us to allow them to settle their account by 90-day Bill of Exchange.

We would be grateful if you could confirm that this company settles promptly on due dates, and are sound enough to (B) credits of up to USD 50,000 in transactions.

Thank you in advance for the information.

31 Who is MOST likely to be Mr. Cho?

① referee

② seller

③ broker

④ drawee

32 Fill in the blank (A) and (B) with right words.

① by – meet   ② from – fill

③ by – grant   ④ from – allow

33 Which of the following words is MOST suitable for the blank below?

Factoring companies provide a flexible and cost effective way to free up capital and improve cash flow. Factoring is a form of (   ) which allow business to raise funds or aid cash flow by providing funds against unpaid invoices. The banks then collect payment from the customer for you, saving you the time and hassle of chasing payments. Once payment is collected, the bank pays the balance of the invoice value, minus agreed fees.

① draft finance

② invoice finance

③ ordering service

④ overdraft service

[34 ~ 35] Read the following and answer.

Dear Herr Kim,

We would like to invite you to our annual dinner on 15 February, and 당신이 우리의 초청 연사 중 한 분이 되어 주실지 궁금합니다.

Our theme this year is 'The effects of the USD', and we would appreciate a contribution from your field on how this is affecting exporting companies.

Please let us know as soon as possible if you are able to speak.

(A) a formal invitation for yourself and a guest.

Yours sincerely,

34 What is best written for the underlined part?

① wonder if you would consider being one of our guest speakers.

② doubt if you would be one of our inviting speaker.

③ want you would accept as one of our speakers.

④ question goes for your acceptance as one of our host speakers.

35 Which is best for the blank (A)?

① Enclosed you will find

② Attached is our file

③ You may put out

④ We appreciate if you could sign

36 Which of the following is the right match for blanks below?

(ⓐ) Average Loss is a voluntary and deliberate loss, while (ⓑ) Average Loss is purely accidental and unforeseen loss. (ⓒ) Average Loss falls entirely upon the owner of the cargo.
In (ⓓ) Average Loss the loss shall be shared by all the owners of cargo.

	ⓐ	ⓑ	ⓒ	ⓓ
①	General	Particular	General	Particular
②	General	Particular	Particular	General
③	Particular	General	General	Particular
④	Particular	General	Particular	General

37 Which is NOT a difference between Institute Cargo Clause(B) and Institute Cargo Clauses(C)?

① Only difference between ICC(B) and ICC(C) is the additional risks covered under ICC(B) cargo insurance policies.

② ICC(C) is the minimum cover cargo insurance policy available in the market.

③ ICC(B) covers loss of or damage to the subject-matter insured caused by entry of sea lake or river water into vessel, craft, hold, conveyance, container or place of storage but ICC(C) does not.

④ ICC(B) covers loss of or damage to the subject-matter insured caused by general average sacrifice but ICC(C) does not.

[38~39] Read the following and answer the questions.

Thank you very much for your letter of March 20th inquiring about our model number HW-118. (a) We have quoted our best prices and terms as attached price list. We trust that you can figure out our eagerness (b) to do business with you as we quoted special prices for you.
As a matter of fact, (c) we may have to raise our prices since (d) the prices of raw materials have been expensive from early this year. Therefore, we would ask you to (e) without delay.

38 Which of the following is grammatically INCORRECT?

① (a)　　② (b)　　③ (c)　　④ (d)

39 Which answer best fits the blank (e)?

① place a backorder

② place an initial order

③ take a bulk order

④ take a volume order

40 Which has the same meaning with the following sentence?

Shipment is to be made within the time stated in the contract, except in circumstances beyond the Seller's control.

① Shipment is to be made within the time without exceptions.

② Shipment is allowed to be made later, if the seller is unable to secure promised materials.

③ The seller is not responsible for delay in shipment in the case of force majeure.

④ The buyer is likely to ignore whatever the seller asks for an excuse.

41 Choose the answer which is MOST similar to the following sentence.

Shipment not later than October 10.

① Shipment anytime after October 10.

② Shipment must be made by October 10.

③ Shipment must be made on October 10.

④ Shipment is no earlier than October 10.

42 Fill in the blank with the best answer.

> Regarding your order number HW-07133, we are pleased to inform you that the goods are ready for shipment.
>
> On such a short notice, please note that we made special effort to meet your required delivery date.
>
> We trust that the excellent quality and the fashionable design of our products will give your customers full satisfaction.
>
> Please let us have your (   ).

① quotation about this order

② letter of credit

③ invoice as soon as possible

④ shipping instructions

[43~46] Which is the most INACCURATE translation in English?

43 ① 선적되어 온 것을 풀어보고 당사는 제품이 귀사의 견본과 품질이 동등하지 않다는 것을 발견하였습니다.

→ While we were unpacking the shipment, we realized that the quality of the goods is not equal to your sample.

② 이 지연으로 말미암아 당사는 큰 불편을 겪었습니다. 더 이상 지연되면 당사는 판매할 기회를 많이 놓친다는 점을 이해해 주십시오.

→ This delay has caused us great disconvenience. You will understand that you would lose much of your chance of selling them if their delivery were put off any further.

③ 귀하께서 당사의 클레임의 타당성을 인정하실 수 있도록 동봉한 견본을 조사해 주시기 바랍니다.

→ We ask you to examine the sample enclosed so that you will admit the reasonableness of our claim.

④ 이 문제를 해결하기 위하여 귀사가 생각하고 있는 할인액을 알려주시기 바랍니다.

→ We would be glad to hear of the allowance you consider in settling this matter.

44 ① 당사는 영국에 거래처가 없으므로 귀사께서 당사가 이 특수 분야의 영업을 할 수 있는 기회를 얻도록 협력해 주신다면 감사하겠습니다.

→ We have no contacts in England, so we would be highly appreciated all the assistance you could render in let us have a chance of doing a business in this particular area.

② 우리들 상호의 이익을 도모하기 위하여 빠른 시일 내에 귀사와 거래를 시작하기를 바랍니다.

→ We hope that we can soon enter into business relations with you which we are sure will lead to our mutual profit.

③ 당사는 서울에 위치한 무역회사로 세계의 주요 무역 중심지에 지점들을 두고 있으며 광범위하고 다양한 상품을 취급하고 있습니다.

→ We are a trading firm in Seoul with branches covering the world's principal trade centers handling a wide range of various goods.

④ 당사는 일반 상품, 기계류 및 장비의 수출입상으로 20년이 넘는 역사를 가지고 있습니다.

→ We have a proud record of more than 20 years in our business as an exporter-importer dealing in general goods, machinery and equipment.

45 ① 보증에 대한 정보도 받아보고 싶습니다.

→ We are also interested in receiving information about the warranty.

② 귀하의 주문품을 오늘 신속히 항공 속달편으로 발송하였습니다.

→ We have today promptly shipped your order by air express.

③ 선적이 지연된 이유는 최근 오클랜드 항구 직원들의 파업 때문입니다.

→ The shipping delay is due to the recent strike of port workers in Oakland.

④ 거듭된 시도에도 불구하고, 귀사로부터 아무런 답변도 받지 못했습니다.

→ Despite of repeated attempts, we have unable to receive an answer from you.

46
① 귀사가 2개월 전 당사에 공급한 배터리에 문제가 있었습니다.
→ There has been a problem with the batteries you had supplied us two months ago.
② 당사 기록을 철저하게 검토한 결과, 추가 금액이 실수로 청구된 것이 확실합니다.
→ Having made a thorough check of our records, I am certain that the extra charge was made in error.
③ 귀사의 22-A01번 주문에 대한 청구서를 보내드린 지 2주가 되었습니다.
→ It was two weeks since we have sent you the billing for your order 22-A01.
④ 사무실 책상과 의자 품목의 사진을 보내주시겠습니까?
→ Would you mind sending me pictures of your line of office desks and chairs?

47 Choose the one which does NOT have the same meaning with the underlined.

> If the payment should not be made, then I am afraid that we shall have no choice but to start proceedings for dishonor.

① resume negotiation
② take a legal step
③ sue
④ bring an action

48 Which is LEAST proper in explanation of Transhipments?

① Transhipments are usually made where there is no direct air, land, or sea link between the consignor's and consignee's countries.
② Transhipments can be made where the intended port of entry is blocked.
③ Transhipments are not allowed in L/C operation, unless the goods are containerised.
④ Transhipments exposes the shipment to a lower probability of damage.

49 What does the underlined mean?

> Underlying transaction is a deal between the account party and beneficiary of a letter of credit(L/C). An L/C is said to be independent of the underlying transaction.

① sales contract
② carriage contract
③ negotiation contract
④ payment terms

50 Which is right for the blank?

> One of the ways how to deal with the negotiation is that the exporter can get a discount from negotiating bank through ( ) for discrepant documents presented under the Documentary Credit.

① under reserve negotiation
② forfaiting
③ factoring
④ confirmation

<제3과목> 무역실무

51 신용장 양도 시 확인사항으로 옳지 않은 것은?
① 2회 이상 양도가능한지 여부
② 원신용장에 명기된 조건대로 양도되는지 여부
③ 당해 L/C가 양도가능(Transferable) 신용장인지 여부
④ 양도은행이 신용장상에 지급, 인수 또는 매입을 하도록 수권 받은 은행인지 여부

52 Incoterms 2010상의 '매도인의 의무(The seller's obligations)'에 관한 항목이 아닌 것은?
① Licences, authorizations, security clearance and other formalities
② Transfer of risks
③ Assistance with information and related costs
④ Provision of goods in conformity with the contract

53 무역계약이 체결된 장소 또는 국가에서 계약의 전부 또는 일부가 이행될 때 계약이 체결된 국가의 법률을 적용해야 한다는 원칙으로 옳은 것은?

① 무명조건
② 계약이행지법
③ 중재지법
④ 계약체결지법

54 다음 설명에 해당하는 수출보증보험의 대상이 되는 보증서는 무엇인가?

> 계약체결 시에 제출하는 것으로서 낙찰자가 약정된 계약을 이행하지 않을 경우에 대비하여 상대방(발주자)이 요구하며 보증금액은 보통 계약금액의 10% 전후이다.

① bid bond
② performance bond
③ advance payment bond
④ retention payment bond

55 다음의 경우 환가료를 원화로 계산한 것으로 옳은 것은?

> 1) 거래금액 : JPY 3,600,000
> 2) 거래조건 : 120d/s
> 3) 환가료율 : 2.00%
> 4) 우편일수 : 8일
> 5) 환율(장부가격) : JPY 100 = KRW 1,000

① 128,000원
② 240,000원
③ 256,000원
④ 480,000원

56 해상운송에 관한 헤이그-비스비 규칙의 설명으로 옳지 않은 것은?

① 운송인의 책임은 과실책임주의에 기초하고 있다.
② 선적 시로부터 양륙시까지의 기간 동안에 대해서만 적용된다.
③ 운송인은 자신에게 과실이 없음을 입증해야만 책임을 면할 수 있다.
④ 운송인은 항해과실에 대해서 책임을 부담하지 않는다.

57 선하증권의 법적 성질로 옳지 않은 것은?

① 요인증권
② 요식증권
③ 상환증권
④ 금전증권

58 신용장에 대한 내용으로 옳지 않은 것은?

① 신용장은 개설은행의 조건부 지급확약으로 상업신용을 은행신용으로 전환시켜 주는 금융수단이다.
② 신용장상에 아무런 언급이 없는 경우 양도가 불가능하다.
③ 무역거래에 일반적으로 사용되는 신용장은 'Documentary Credit'이다.
④ 신용장에 의해 발행되는 환어음의 만기가 'at 90 days after sight'라면 'Sight Credit'이 된다.

59 해상운송 과정 중에 발생한 해상사고로 화물손해가 발생하였고, surveyor의 조사결과 general average에 해당하지 않는 사고로 판명되었다. 이 경우 화주가 손해를 보상받을 수 있는 해상적화보험조건으로 구성된 것은?

① ICC(A), ICC(B)
② ICC(A), ICC(C)
③ ICC(B), ICC(C)
④ ICC(A), ICC(B), ICC(C)

60 정기선의 해상운임에 대한 설명으로 옳지 않은 것은?

① 정기선의 해상운임은 기본운임(Basic Rates)에 할증료(Surcharges), 추가요금(Additional Charges) 등으로 구성된다.
② 품목별무차별운임(Freight All Kinds, FAK)은 품목에 관계없이 동일하게 적용하는 운임이다.
③ BAF는 유류할증료, CAF는 통화할증료로 운임 외에 부가되는 할증료(Surcharge)이다.
④ THC는 터미널화물처리비를 말하는데 통상적으로 해상운임에 포함되어 있다.

61 중재합의에 대한 설명으로 옳지 않은 것은?

① 유효한 중재합의가 존재하는 경우에는 직소금지의 원칙에 따라 소송으로 분쟁을 해결할 수가 없다.

② 분쟁 발생 후에도 중재합의는 별도의 중재계약에 의해 이루어질 수 있다.

③ 우리나라 중재법에 따르면 중재합의는 서면으로 하여야 한다.

④ 중재합의의 한 형태로서 매매계약서상에 삽입되어 있는 중재조항은 동 계약서가 무효가 되면 동 중재조항도 그 효력을 자동적으로 상실하게 된다.

62. Incoterms 2010에 대한 설명으로 옳지 않은 것은?

① Incoterms 2010은 국내매매계약에도 사용가능하다.

② EXW에서 매도인은 물품을 매수인의 운송수단에 적입할 의무가 없다.

③ 컨테이너 운송에서는 FOB나 CIF 조건은 부적절하다.

④ FAS 조건에서 매도인은 외항에 정박한 본선까지의 부선료를 부담할 필요가 없다.

63 원신용장을 견질로 하여 국내의 공급업자 앞으로 개설하는 내국신용장에 대한 설명으로 옳지 않은 것은?

① 내국신용장상에서는 표시통화는 원화, 외화, 원화 및 외화금액 부기 중 하나이어야 한다.

② 유효기일은 물품의 인도기일에 최장 10일을 가산한 기일 이내이어야 한다.

③ 부가가치세 영세율을 적용한다.

④ 어음 형식은 개설의뢰인을 지급인으로 하고, 개설은행을 지급장소로 하는 기한부 환어음이어야 한다.

64 매도인 계약위반과 매수인 권리구제에 대한 설명으로 옳지 않은 것은?

① 매도인이 계약을 이행하지 않는 경우에 매수인은 원칙적으로 계약대로의 이행을 청구할 수 있다.

② 매수인은 매도인의 의무이행을 위하여 추가기간을 지정할 수 없다.

③ 매수인이 수령당시와 동등한 상태로 반환할 수 없는 경우에는 대체물품인도 청구권을 상실한다.

④ 계약의 해제는 정당한 손해배상의무를 제외하고는 당사자 쌍방을 모든 계약상의 의무로부터 해방시킨다.

65 승인조건부 청약이나 보세창고도거래 등에서 품질을 결정하는데 가장 바람직한 방법은?

① 표준품매매   ② 상표매매

③ 명세서매매   ④ 점검매매

66 Incoterms 2010상 FCA 조건에 대한 설명으로 옳지 않은 것은?

① 매도인은 매수인이 지정한 장소(수출국 내륙의 한 지점)에서 매수인이 지정한 운송인에게 물품 인도

② 인도장소가 매도인의 구내인 경우, 매수인의 집화용 차량에 적재하여 인도

③ 인도장소가 매도인의 구내 이외의 장소인 경우, 물품을 적재한 차량을 매수인이 지정한 장소에 반입함으로써 인도(반입된 차량으로부터 양륙할 의무는 없음)

④ 매도인이 지정 운송인에 인도한 물품에 대해 매수인이 수출통관의무 부담

67 무역계약에서 수량조건에 대한 설명으로 옳지 않은 것은?

① 수량을 표시하는 용어는 Piece, Length, Measurement, weight, package 등이 있다.

② 용적을 표시하는 용어는 CBM, TEU, Liter, Square, Drum 등이 있다.

③ 중량 1톤을 영국계에서는 1,016kg, 미국계는 907kg이며 유럽계는 1,000kg으로 사용한다.

④ UCP 600에는 산화물의 과부족 용인에 대해 어음발행 금액이 신용장금액을 초과하지 않는 범위 내에서 5%의 과부족을 허용하는 규정을 두고 있다.

68 운임에 관한 설명으로 옳지 않은 것은?

① Port Congestion Surcharge – 도착항에 체선(滯船)이 있어 선박의 가동률이 저하되는 경우에 발생하는 선사의 손해를 화주에게 전가하기 위하여 부과하는 할증요금

② Bunker Adjustment Factor – 선박의 연료인 벙커유의 가격변동에 따른 손실을 보전하기 위하여 부과하는 할증요금

③ Lump Sum Charge – 적재할 때에 지정하였던 양륙항을 선적 후에 변경할 경우에 추가로 부과되는 운임

④ Transhipment Charge – 화주가 환적을 요청하는 경우에 선사가 그에 따른 추가비용을 보전하기 위하여 부과하는 운임

69 Incoterms 2010의 사용법에 대한 내용으로 옳지 않은 것은?

① Incoterms 2010 규칙을 적용하고자 하는 경우, 그러한 취지를 계약에서 명확히 하여야 한다.

② 선택된 Incoterms 규칙은 당해 물품과 운송방법에 적합한 것이어야 한다.

③ Incoterms 규칙은 매매대금이나 그 지급방법 등과 관련 매도인과 매수인의 부담을 명확히 규정하고 있다.

④ Incoterms 규칙보다 국내법의 강행규정이 우선한다.

70 해상화물을 컨테이너 방식으로 선적할 때 이에 대한 설명으로 옳지 않은 것은?

① 운송계약의 청약에 해당하는 선복요청서와 승낙에 해당하는 인수확인서에 의해서 실제적인 운송계약이 성립한다.

② FCL 화물인 경우에 수출상의 공장 또는 창고에서 화주의 책임하에 컨테이너에 화물을 적재한다.

③ 구체적인 선적일정에 의해 본선이 입항하면 컨테이너는 CY에서 마샬링야드(Marshalling Yard)로 이송되어 본선적재가 이루어진다.

④ LCL 화물인 경우 화물인수도증을 근거로 운송주선인은 개별화주에게 Master B/L을 발급해 줄 수 있다.

71 무역운송을 이해하는 데 가장 기초를 이루는 해상운송에 대한 설명으로 옳지 않은 것은?

① 해상운송계약은 정기선에 의한 개품운송계약과 부정기선에 의한 용선운송계약으로 나눈다.

② 개품운송에 사용되는 운송서류로는 선하증권과 해상화물운송장이 있다.

③ 용선자가 제3자의 화물을 운송하는 경우에 화주에게 용선계약부 선하증권을 발급해 줄 수 있다.

④ 신용장이 용선계약부 선하증권과 관련하여 용선계약서 제시를 요구하는 경우에는 은행은 반드시 용선계약서를 심사해야 한다.

72 개별계약과 포괄계약의 내용 및 상호관계에 대한 설명이다. (ⓐ), (ⓑ), (ⓒ)안에 들어갈 용어로 올바르게 연결한 것은?

> 개별계약서에는 (ⓐ) 등을 명기한다. 포괄계약서에는 (ⓑ) 등이 명기된다. 포괄계약과 개별계약은 상호 보완적이며, 서로 모순될 경우 (ⓒ) 내용이 우선한다.

① ⓐ 단가, ⓑ 청약 및 주문의 방식, ⓒ 개별계약

② ⓐ 청약 및 주문의 방식, ⓑ 선적일의 증명방법, ⓒ 개별계약

③ ⓐ 인도시기, ⓑ 수량, ⓒ 포괄계약

④ ⓐ 품명, ⓑ 불가항력조항, ⓒ 포괄계약

73 리네고(재매입)가 발생할 수 있는 신용장으로 올바르게 짝지은 것은?

> ㉠ available with JAKARTA BANK by SIGHT PAYMENT
> ㉡ available with JAKARTA BANK by ACCEPTANCE
> ㉢ available with JAKARTA BANK by DEFERRED PAYMENT
> ㉣ available with ANY BANK by NEGOTIATION
> ㉤ available with JAKARTA BANK by NEGOTIATION

① ㉠, ㉢, ㉣   ② ㉡, ㉢, ㉤

③ ㉢, ㉣, ㉤   ④ ㉡, ㉣, ㉤

74 송화인의 요구에 따라 항공사, 송화인 또는 대리인이 선불한 비용을 수화인으로부터 징수하는 금액은?

① THC

② CFS Charge

③ Documentation Fee

④ Disbursement Fee

75 청약의 요건으로 옳지 않은 것은?

① 1인 혹은 그 이상의 특정인에 대한 의사표시일 것

② 물품의 표시, 대금 및 수량에 관하여 충분히 확정적인 의사표시일 것

③ 승낙이 있는 경우 이에 구속된다는 의사표시가 있을 것

④ 상대방의 거래문의에 대한 응답으로 절대적이고 무조건적인 거래개설의 의사표시

<제1과목> 영문해석

01 Which is related to "offer subject to prior sale"?

① We are pleased to offer firm subject to receiving your reply by September 30, 2018.

② We are pleased to offer you the following items subject to our final confirmation.

③ We have the pleasure in offering you the following items subject to being unsold.

④ We have the pleasure in offering you the following items subject to receiving your reply by September 30, 2018.

02 Which deals with a different topic from others?

① We would only be prepared to supply on a cash basis.

② Our factory does not have facilities to turn out 30,000 units a week.

③ The shirts we manufacture are sold by the dozen in one colour. I regret that we never sell individual garments.

④ Our factory only sells material in 30-meter rolls which cannot be cut up.

03 Which is most awkward when it is used in closing part of the business letter?

① We hope that this will be the first of many orders we place with you.

② We will place further orders if this one is completed to our satisfaction.

③ If our sales targets are met, we shall be placing further orders in near future.

④ The carpets should be wrapped, and the packaging reinforced at both ends to avoid wear.

04 Which has a different topic from others?

① It is essential that the goods should be delivered in time before the beginning of November for the Christmas sales period.

② Delivery before 28 February is a firm condition of this order, and we reserve the right to refuse goods delivered after that time.

③ Please confirm that you can complete the work before the end of March, as the opening of the store is planned for early April.

④ We would like to confirm that the 25% trade discount is quite satisfactory.

05 What does the following refer to?

> The shipper is liable to pay freight if the goods shipped are carried, on his instructions or in his interest, to a place other than the port of destination.

① Dead freight   ② Lump sum freight

③ Put option freight   ④ Back freight

06 Which is WRONG in the explanation of CIP under Incoterms 2010?

① The seller must contract or procure a contract for the carriage of the goods from the agreed point of destination.

② The contract of carriage must be made on usual terms at the seller's expense and provide for carriage by the usual route and in a customary manner.

③ The seller must obtain at its own expense cargo insurance at least with the minimum cover.

④ The buyer must pay the costs of any mandatory pre-shipment inspection, except when such inspection is mandated by the authorities of the country of export.

07 What is WRONG in the explanation of Incoterms 2010?

① DAT requires the seller to bear all transportation-related costs and risks up to the delivery point at the agreed destination, which may be in the buyer's country.

② CPT requires the seller to clear the goods for export, where applicable. However, the seller has no obligation to clear the goods for import, pay any import duty.

③ FOB requires the seller to deliver the goods on board the vessel or to procure goods already so delivered for shipment.

④ CIF requires the parties to specify the port of destination, which is where risk passes to the buyer.

08 Which of the following is NOT appropriate as shipping documents when presented for the negotiation of L/C under FCA term?

① On board Bill of Lading

② Commercial Invoice

③ Forwarder's Cargo Receipt

④ Packing list

[09 ~ 10] Read the following and answer.

Dear Mr. Merton,

Please find attached an order(R1432) from our principals, Mackenzie Bros Ltd, 1-5 Whale Drive, Dawson, Ontario, Canada.

They have asked us to instruct you that the 60 sets of crockery ordered should be packed in 6 crates, 10 sets per crate, with each piece individually wrapped, and the crates marked clearly with their name, the words 'fragile' and 'crockery', and numbered 1-6.

Please send any further correspondence relating to shipment or payment direct to Mackenzie Bros, and let us have a copy of the commercial invoice when it is made up.

Many thanks,

David Han

09 Who might be Mackenzie Bros Ltd?

① buyer

② seller

③ freight forwarder

④ carrier

10 Why does David Han want a copy of commercial invoice?

① to calculate an agent commission to be charged to the Mackenzie Bros Ltd later.

② to ask an agent commission to Mr. Merton after supply of goods.

③ to keep it as a record for principal.

④ to calculate import tax for his customer.

11 What is NOT obligation of seller according to CISG?

① delivery of the goods

② hand over any documents relating to the delivery

③ transfer the property in the goods

④ examine the goods after arrival

12 What does the following refer to?

A document required by certain foreign countries for usually tariff purposes, certifying the country in which specified goods have been manufactured, processed, or produced in the exporting country.

① Commercial Invoice

② Bill of Exchange

③ Bill of Lading

④ Certificate of Origin

13 Choose one that is NOT correct about the remedies regulated in the CISG(United Nation Convention on Contracts for the International Sale of Goods).

① The buyer may require the delivery of substitute goods only when non-conformity constitutes a fundamental breach of contract.

② The buyer may require to repair the goods only when non-conformity constitutes a fundamental breach of contract.

③ When non-delivery of goods constitutes a fundamental breach of goods, the buyer may declare avoidance of contract.

④ The buyer may claim for damage even when non-conformity does not constitute a fundamental breach of contract.

14 Which of the following statements on the documentary credit under UCP 600 is CORRECT?

① It is an undertaking enforceable against the advising bank even if the issuing bank is unable to pay.

② It is an undertaking enforceable against the applicant even if the issuing bank is unwilling to pay.

③ It is a guarantee enforceable against the nominated bank even if the issuing bank is willing to pay.

④ It is an irrevocable undertaking enforceable against the issuing bank even if the confirming bank is unwilling to pay.

15 Which is NOT correct about order B/L?

① It is negotiable transport document.

② When it is issued "TO ORDER", the buyer may endorse.

③ The cargo may be transferred ONLY to the party to whom the bill of lading has been endorsed.

④ The cargo may be released when at least 1 of the issued originals is surrendered.

16 In accordance with UCP 600, which of the following terms may NOT be reduced or curtailed on a transferred documentary credit?

① the amount of the credit

② any unit price

③ the latest shipment date

④ the percentage for which insurance cover must be effected

17 Which is correct about Bill of Exchange?

> (a) It is used only in international trade.
> (b) Draft is another name for Bill of Exchange.
> (c) It is used as a payment guarantee.
> (d) Drawee under negotiation L/C is applicant.

① (a)　　② (b)　　③ (c)　　④ (d)

[18~19] Read the following and answer the questions.

> Dear Mr. Brown,
> We thank you very much for your inquiry of July 5th and are glad to hear that you are interested in our products.
> In your letter, you requested a special price discount of 5% off the list prices. While appreciating your interest in our products, we have to point out that we have already cut our prices to the minimum possible and that these goods are not obtainable elsewhere at these prices.
> However, 'in case' you are ready to increase your order for over 100,000 pieces at a time, please be advised that we can allow you quantity discount of 5% as you requested.
> Sincerely yours,
> Mike Son

18 Which does NOT have similar meaning to 'in case'?

① in spite   ② provided

③ if   ④ when

19 Which is MOST appropriate about the letter?

① Mr. Brown asked Mike Son to raise the price.

② The writer accepts Mr. Brown's offer.

③ Mike Son is a buyer.

④ Mike Son suggests a volume discount.

20 Which of the followings words is NOT appropriate for the blanks below?

> Under the letter of credit transaction, bill of lading is consigned directly "to order" or "to the order of" a designated party, usually (ⓐ) or (ⓑ).
> The phrase "to order" or "to the order of (ⓐ)" signifies (ⓒ) permitting the title of the merchandise to be transferred many times by means of appropriate (ⓓ).

① ⓐ the shipper   ② ⓑ the buyer

③ ⓒ "negotiable"   ④ ⓓ endorsement

21 Which of the following is LEAST proper about the letter?

> Dear Mr. Steve,
> We are obliged for your letter of 22nd May quoting for "Kleenkwick" cleaning powder at USD 9,000 per case, but regret that at this price we cannot place an order. If your prices are within our reach, we could place regular large orders.
> We therefore hope you will reconsider your quotation and find it possible to offer a lower price, calculated on the basis of a monthly order for a minimum of forty cases.
> Your faithfully,
> Grace Yang

① Mr. Steve have sent a quotation to Grace before, and the price is a bit higher than what Grace expected.

② Grace asks to lower the price.

③ Mr. Steve expresses regret at inability to accept.

④ Grace may make a firm offer if the price is lowered.

22 The following is a part of the contract. Which document is MOST appropriate for transport under the price terms?

> Description : TV Monitors (Item No. 123 - ABS)
> Quantity : 2,000 pcs
> Price : USD 200/pcs FCA Daejeon
> Place of Destination : New York

① Multimodal Transport Bill of Lading

② Air Waybill

③ Ocean Bill of Lading

④ Inland Waterway Transport Document

23 Which of the following is NOT appropriate as the obligation of the buyer under FCA term of Incoterms 2010?

① Payment of all costs relating to the goods from the time they have been delivered by the seller.

② Payment of any additional costs incurred by failing to take delivery of the goods when they have been placed at the buyer's disposal.

③ Payment of the costs of carrying out customs formalities payable upon import.

④ Reimburse all costs incurred by the seller in loading the goods at the seller's premises.

24 Which of the following is the payment method involved?

> This is to notify you that the goods invoiced by you on December 12 have arrived here. In settlement of the amount of invoice, Korea Exchange Bank accepted your bill of exchange, for USD 35,800 at 120 days after sight together with shipping documents. The proceeds will be sent to you at maturity accordingly.

① Deferred payment credit
② Standby credit
③ Usance credit
④ D/P

25 Which of the following is LEAST appropriate about the letter?

> Dear Mr. Kirchoffer:
> This is the third time we have called your attention to your long-overdue account. So far we have received neither your check nor the courtesy of a reply.
> Credit and friendly relations are complementary efforts. We feel we have done our part and are counting on you as a fair-minded businessman to meet your obligations. Please send your check by this week. Otherwise, we will take a legal action.
> Sincerely,
> Anthony T. Legere

① Kirchoffer's account has long been past due.
② Anthony has sent several reminders to Kirchoffer requesting payment.
③ Kirchoffer replied to Anthony but did not send the check.
④ This is a stern ultimatum for collection.

<제2과목> 영작문

26 What is the seller's DDP price under the followingcost break down? (excluding optional cost)

> Cost of Goods : USD 100
> freight : USD 10
> Insurance : USD 5
> Export TAX : USD 5
> THC in Seller's country : USD 5
> Import TAX : USD 5

① USD 125   ② USD 130
③ USD 120   ④ USD 115

[27~28] Read the following and answer.

> Dear Mr Couper,
>
> The above order has now been completed and sent to Busan Port where it is awaiting to be loaded on to the SS Arirang, sailing for London on 06 July and arriving on 30 July. When we have the necessary documents, we will forward them to (A) Seoul Bank, here, and they will forward them to HSBC London for collection.
>
> We have taken particular care to see that the goods have been packed (   ) your instructions: the six crates have been marked with your name.
>
> If you need any further information, please contact us.
>
> Yours sincerely,
> Peter Han

27 What role may (A) Seoul Bank assume if D/A is employed as payment?

① Remitting Bank   ② Advising Bank
③ Collecting Bank   ④ Confirming Bank

28 Fill in the blank with suitable word.

① as per   ② regarding

③ with reference   ④ into

29 Which word fits best for the blanks?

> Dear Simon Lee,
>
> I intend to place a substantial order with you in the next few months.
>
> As you know, over the past two years I have placed a number of orders with you and settled promptly, so I hope this has established my reputation with your company. Nevertheless, if necessary, I am willing to supply (   ).
>
> I would like, if possible, to settle future accounts every three months with payments (   ) quarterly statements.

① credits – for

② references – against

③ credits – against

④ debits – from

30 What is the name of the surcharge?

> Apart from normal freight, an additional surcharge is levied by shipping company to cover a foreign exchange loss from the fluctuation of exchange rate of the currency of its own country and US Dollars in which freight is paid.

① CAF   ② BAF

③ IAF   ④ Currency Surcharge

[31 ~ 32] Read the following and answer.

> I have enclosed an order No.1555 for seven more 'SleepAid' beds which have proved to be a popular (   ) here, and will pay for them as usual <u>on invoice</u>. However, I wondered if in future you would let me settle my accounts by monthly statement as this would be more convenient for me.
>
> As we have been dealing with one another for some time, I hope you will agree to trade on the basis of (   ) facilities.
>
> Yours sincerely,

31 What does the underlined 'on invoice' imply?

① settlement by cash

② payment by sight LC

③ payment by sight draft

④ settlement by open account

32 Fill in the blanks with suitable words.

① products – escrow account

② line – open account

③ offer – escrow account

④ agenda – open account

[33 ~ 34] Read the following and answer.

> Dear Mr Cooper,
>
> We wrote to you on two occasions, 21 October and 14 November, concerning the above account, which now has an outstanding balance of USD 3,541.46 and is made up of the <u>copy invoices</u> enclosed.
>
> We have waited three months for (   ) a reply to explain why the balance has not been cleared, (   ) a remittance, but have received (   ).
>
> We are reluctant to take legal action to recover the amount, but you leave us no alternative. Unless we receive your remittance within the next ten days, we will instruct our solicitors to start proceedings.
>
> Yours sincerely,

33 Choose best words for the blanks.

① either - or - neither

② neither - nor - either

③ either - and - neither

④ neither - and - either

34 Why did the writer enclose the 'copy invoices'?

① To request double payment

② Copy invoices prove better than original invoices

③ To back up original invoices sent previously

④ Copy invoice is more cost saving over original invoice

35 Fill in the blank with a suitable word.

> Letter of Indemnity is issued by a merchandise shipper to a steamship company as an inducement for the carrier to issue a clean bill of lading, where it might not otherwise do so, and this document serves as a form of guarantee whereby the shipper agrees to settle a claim against the line by a (   ) of the bill of lading arising from issuance of a clean bill.

① carrier   ② grantor

③ consignor   ④ holder

36 What is THIS?

> THIS is the term used to describe the offence of trying to conceal money that has been obtained through offences such as drug trafficking.
>
> In other words, money obtained from certain crimes, such as extortion, insider trading, drug trafficking and illegal gambling is "dirty".

① money laundering

② fraud

③ illegal investment

④ abnormal remittance

37 Choose the WRONG English composition for Korean meaning.

> 당사의 정보에 따르면, 해당 상사는 제때에 채무를 변제하고 있습니다.

① According to our records, they are punctually meeting their credits.

② As far as our information goes, they are punctually meeting their liabilities.

③ According to our records, they are punctually meeting their commitments.

④ As far as our information goes, they are punctually meeting their obligations.

38 Which of the following statements on forfaiting is NOT correct?

① It helps exporters to obtain cash flow by selling their receivables with a discounted price to forfaiting companies.

② Forfaiting can be applied to a wide range of trade related and purely financial receivables.

③ Forfaiting can be applied to both international and domestic transactions.

④ Under a forfaiting agreement, 100% financing is made with recourse to the seller of the debt.

39 Which of the following statements on the UCP 600 is NOT correct?

① The UCP 600 rules are voluntarily incorporated into contracts and have to be specifically outlined in trade finance contracts when LC is used for finance.

② An accompaniment to the UCP 600 is the ISBP, which assists with understanding whether a document complies with the terms of Letters of Credit.

③ UCP 600 rules apply to any documentary credit except for the standby letter of credit.

④ Credits that are issued and governed by UCP 600 will be interpreted in line with the entire articles contained in UCP 600. However, exceptions to the rules can be made by express modification or exclusion.

40 Considering Incoterms 2010, which of the following statement is NOT correct about the case below?

> Consider goods that are taken in charge at Felixstowe, UK, for transport to Long Beach, California, under the rule "CIP Long Beach, California, Incoterms 2010".

① The seller will arrange and pay for freight to Long Beach.

② The seller will arrange and pay for the export clearance.

③ The buyer will arrange and pay for the inland transportation to his premise in the importing country.

④ The risk will pass from the seller to the buyer upon delivery of the goods to the carrier at Long Beach.

41 Which of the following is LEAST appropriate?

> Thank you very much for your samples and price list of silk fabrics we received today.
> (a) Upon inspecting them, we appreciate the excellence of your products in both material and finish, but we have to tell you that (b) your prices are substantially high compared with those of Italian origin.
> We are afraid that (c) there is little chance of doing business with you (d) unless five percent discount off your list prices is not granted.

① (a)　　　　　② (b)

③ (c)　　　　　④ (d)

42 Which of the following words is NOT appropriate for the blanks below?

> One of the most common mistakes in using Incoterms rules is the use of a traditional "sea and inland waterway only" rule such as (ⓐ) for containerized goods, instead of the "all transport modes" rule (ⓑ). This has exposed the exporter to unnecessary risks. A dramatic recent example was the Japanese tsunami in March 2011, which wrecked the Sendai container terminal. Many hundreds of consignments awaiting despatch were damaged. Exporters who were using (ⓒ) found themselves responsible for losses that could have been avoided!
> Another common mistake is attempting to use (ⓓ) without thinking through whether the seller can undertake all the necessary formalities in the buyer's country, such as paying GST or VAT.

① ⓐ FOB　　　　② ⓑ FCA

③ ⓒ FCA　　　　④ ⓓ DDP

[43 ~ 44] Read the following and answer.

> Dear Mr Cupper,
>
> I am sorry that at present I am unable to settle your invoice dated 9 May for your invoice No. 1555. The reason for this is that our stockroom was flooded after recent heavy rain, and much of the stock were damaged or destroyed.
>
> Unfortunately, I am unable to pay any of my suppliers until I receive compensation from my ( ). They have promised me this within the next four weeks. As soon as I receive payment, I will settle the invoice in full.
>
> I hope that you will understand the situation.
>
> Yours sincerely

43 What is the main purpose of this letter?

① Request for more time to settle a debt

② Explain why suppliers do not meet compensation

③ Chase payments for unsettled account

④ Ask claims to insurance company

44 Fill in the blank with right word(s).

① Insurer

② Insurance policy holder

③ Surveyor

④ Insured

45 Which of the following is a correct set of words for the blanks at the message below?

Both letter of credit(L/C) and bill of exchange (B/E) facilitate international transactions between buyers and sellers. The main difference between the two is that a (ⓐ) is a payment mechanism whereas a (ⓑ) is a payment instrument.

The (ⓒ) will set up the conditions that are to be met in order for the payment to be made, and is not the actual payment itself. On the other hand, a (ⓓ) is a payment instrument where the seller can discount the (ⓔ) with the bank and receive payment. At maturity, the (ⓕ) will become a negotiable payment instrument that can be traded, and the holder of the (ⓖ) (either the seller or the bank) will receive payment.

	ⓐ	ⓑ	ⓒ	ⓓ	ⓔ	ⓕ	ⓖ
①	L/C	B/E	B/E	L/C	B/E	B/E	L/C
②	L/C	B/E	L/C	B/E	B/E	B/E	B/E
③	B/E	L/C	L/C	B/E	B/E	B/E	L/C
④	B/E	L/C	B/E	L/C	B/E	B/E	B/E

46 Fill in the blank with right expression.

Your order No. 1555 is being sent express rail-freight and can be delivered after 09:00 tomorrow.

Enclosed is consignment note No.051202, which should be presented on delivery. You should contact us immediately if any problems arise.

Thank you for your order, and we hope ( ) in the future.

Yours faithfully,

① we can be of further service

② the problem is sorted out soon

③ an enhanced credit allowance

④ an extended credit period

47 Choose the WRONG word for each blank.

Draft means a written order by the first party, called the (ⓐ), instructing a second party, called the (ⓑ)(such as the bank), to pay money to a third party, called the (ⓒ). An order to pay a sum certain in money, signed by a drawer, payable on (ⓓ) or at a definite time.

① ⓐ drawer   ② ⓑ drawee

③ ⓒ payee   ④ ⓓ future

48 Choose the WRONG part from (a) ~ (d).

(a) Stranding means the drifting, driving, or running aground of a ship on a shore or strand. (b) This term includes bumping over a bar, a mere touch and go or a grounding (c) by reason of the rise and fall of the tide. (d) The vessel must be hard and fast for a appreciable period of time.

① (a)   ② (b)   ③ (c)   ④ (d)

49 Fill in the blank (ⓐ) and (ⓑ) with right word(s).

> Where the insurance policy specifies the extent of value of the insured property, the policy is called a(n) (ⓐ) and where the insurance policy does not show or declare the subject-matter insured, the policy is called the (ⓑ).

① ⓐ floating policy, ⓑ valued policy
② ⓐ valued policy, ⓑ time policy
③ ⓐ unvalued policy, ⓑ valued policy
④ ⓐ valued policy, ⓑ floating policy

50 Which of the following statements on 'transferable credit' is NOT appropriate?

① A transferable credit may be made available in whole or in part to another beneficiary ("second beneficiary") at the request of the beneficiary ("first beneficiary").
② Transferring bank means a nominated bank that transfers the credit or, in a credit available with any bank, a bank that is specifically authorized by the issuing bank to transfer and that transfers the credit.
③ Unless otherwise agreed at the time of transfer all charges (such as commissions, fees, costs or expenses) incurred in respect of a transfer must be paid by the issuing bank.
④ Transferred credit means a credit that has been made available by the transferring bank to a second beneficiary.

<제3과목> 무역실무

51 화인(shipping marking) 가운데 표시되어야 할 필수사항으로 옳지 않은 것은?

① 주화인(main mark)
② 화번(case number)
③ 항구표시(port mark)
④ 주의표시(attention mark)

52 CISG상 일방당사자의 청약 의사표시가 충분히 확정적이기 위한 요건으로 옳지 않은 것은?

① 물품을 표시하고 있을 것
② 대금을 정하고 있거나 이를 정하는 규정을 두고 있을 것
③ 수량을 정하고 있거나 이를 정하는 규정을 두고 있을 것
④ 분쟁해결방법을 정하고 있거나 이를 정하는 규정을 두고 있을 것

53 해상보험에서 물적손해(Physical Loss)에 대한 설명으로 옳지 않은 것은?

① 현실전손은 보험의 목적이 파괴(destroyed)된 경우 또는 물적으로 존재하고 있지만 보험에 부보된 종류의 물품으로서 존재할 수 없을 정도로 심한 경우를 말한다.
② 추정전손은 현실전손은 아니지만 보험목적물을 구조하기 위한 비용과 구조 후의 수리비용이 보험목적 가액을 초과하여 경제적 전손이라고 인정되는 경우가 해당된다.
③ 추정전손은 위부의 행위를 수반하게 되는데 보험목적물의 일부에 대해서도 위부가 가능하다.
④ 공동해손이란 선박이나 화물이 해난에 직면하였을 때 선박 및 화물을 위험으로부터 구조하기 위하여 선장이 임의적으로, 그리고 합리적으로 선박이나 화물의 일부를 희생시키거나 비용을 지출함으로서 발생한 분손을 말한다.

54 수출환변동과 수입환변동 두 제도의 비교 설명으로 옳지 않은 것은?

	구 분	수출환변동	수입환변동
①	가입목적	환율상승에 따른 손실방지	환율하락에 따른 손실방지
②	가입기업	수출기업	수입기업
③	보험금지급 (K-sure→기업)	환율 하락 시	환율 상승 시
④	이익금환수 (기업→K-sure)	환율 상승 시	환율 하락 시

55 Incoterms 2010상 CPT(Carriage Paid To)에 대한 설명으로 옳지 않은 것은?

① 매도인은 해상운송서류를 제공할 필요가 없으며, 해당되는 운송방식에서 통상적으로 사용되는 운송서류를 제공하면 된다.

② 매도인은 물품의 적재비를 포함하여 목적지까지의 운송계약에 따른 비용과 운반비를 부담해야 한다.

③ 매수인은 목적지에서 양하비가 운송비에 포함되어 있지 아니할 경우 이를 지급해야 한다.

④ 매수인은 매도인에 대한 통지 불이행으로 인하여 물품의 인도가 지연되어 발생하는 모든 위험과 추가적인 비용을 지급할 필요가 없다.

56 무역계약의 품질조건에 대한 설명으로 옳지 않은 것은?

① 선적품질조건에는 EXW, FAS, FCA, FOB 조건이 속한다.

② 선적품질조건에는 Tale Quale, FAQ가 속한다.

③ 양륙품질조건에는 CFR, CIF, CPT, CIP, DAT, DAP, DDU, DDP 조건이 속한다.

④ 양륙품질조건에는 Rye Term, GMQ가 속한다.

57 도착항의 항만사정이 선박으로 혼잡할 경우 신속히 하역할 수 없고, 선박의 가동률이 저하되어 선박 회사에 손해가 발생하므로 이를 화주에게 전가하는 정기선 운임의 할증료를 무엇이라 하는가?

① 장척할증료 ② 항만변경료
③ 체화할증료 ④ 환적할증료

58 환어음의 필수기재사항에 해당하는 것은?

① 지급인 – 지급기일 – 수취인 – 발행일 및 발행지

② 환어음표시문자 – 지급인 – 지급지 – 신용장 번호

③ 금액 – 지급지 – 어음번호 – 발행인의 서명

④ 상환불능문언 – 환어음표시문자 – 발행인의 서명 – 환율문언

59 해상운송에서 정기선 운송과 부정기선 운송을 비교한 내용으로 옳지 않은 것은?

① 부정기선 운송은 미리 정해진 항로가 없다.

② 정기선 운송은 미리 공시된 운임률표에 따라 운임이 결정된다.

③ 정기선 운송의 화물은 완제품 내지 반제품이 주종을 이루지만, 부정기선의 화물은 원자재나 농·광산물이 주종을 이룬다.

④ 부정기선의 운임은 물동량(수요)과 선복(공급)에 영향을 받지 않는다.

60 무역계약의 계약자유원칙에 대한 내용으로 옳지 않은 것은?

① 계약체결의 자유
② 불평등초래 약관을 포함한 계약내용 결정의 자유
③ 계약체결방식의 자유
④ 계약 상대방 선택의 자유

61 신용장에 대한 내용으로 옳지 않은 것은?

① 신용장에서 단순히 "Invoice"라고만 표기된 경우, 송장상에 서명이 없어도 된다.

② 신용장에서 단순히 "Invoice"라고만 표기된 경우, 송장상에 발행일자가 없어도 된다.

③ 신용장에서 복합운송증권을 요구하는 경우 B/L 명칭도 사용 가능하다.

④ 신용장에서 복합운송증권을 요구하는 경우 Charter Party B/L도 사용 가능하다.

62 Transferable Credit에 대한 설명으로 옳은 것은?

① L/C상에 "transferable" 등 양도가 가능하다는 표현이 없어도 가능하다.

② L/C 금액의 전부를 transfer하는 전액양도만 허용된다.

③ 2nd Beneficiary가 3rd Beneficiary에게 양도하는 경우 Applicant의 사전 양해를 얻는다면 가능하다.

④ 국내는 물론 국외에 소재하고 있는 2nd Beneficiary에게도 양도가 가능하다.

63 (ⓐ), (ⓑ), (ⓒ) 안에 들어갈 용어로 옳은 것은?

(ⓐ)조건은 선적지인도조건이기 때문에 계약에 별도의 명시가 없으면 선적 시를 품질기준시기로 보아야 한다. 곡물류의 거래에 있어서 (ⓑ)는 선적품질조건을 의미하며 (ⓒ)는 조건부 선적품질조건으로 해상운송 중 생긴 유손(damaged by wet) 등으로 야기되는 품질손해에 대하여는 매도인이 도착 시까지 책임을 지는 조건이다.

① ⓐ FCA, ⓑ TQ(tale quale), ⓒ SD(sea damage)
② ⓐ CPT, ⓑ RT(rye term), ⓒ SD(sea damage)
③ ⓐ DAP, ⓑ SD(sea damage), ⓒ RT(rye term)
④ ⓐ CIF, ⓑ TQ(tale quale), ⓒ RT(rye term)

64 수출 컨테이너화물의 선적 시 진행순서를 옳게 나열한 것은?

① Booking Note → S/R → B/L → EIR → Dock's Receipt

② EIR → S/R → B/L → Booking Note → Dock's Receipt

③ S/R → Booking Note → EIR → Dock's Receipt → B/L

④ EIR → S/R → Dock's Receipt → B/L → Booking Note

65 "freight forwarder"가 하는 역할로 옳지 않은 것은?

① Customs brokerage provider

② Port agent

③ Inspector

④ Multimodal transport operator

66 UCP 600에서 Honour의 의미에 해당되지 않는 것은?

① 신용장이 일람지급으로 이용이 가능하다면 일람출금으로 지급하는 것

② 신용장이 연지급으로 이용이 가능하다면 연지급을 확약하고 만기에 지급하는 것

③ 신용장이 매입으로 이용이 가능하면 환어음 및 서류를 매수하는 것

④ 신용장이 인수에 의해서 이용이 가능하다면 수익자가 발행한 환어음을 인수하고 만기에 지급하는 것

67 중재제도에 관한 다음 설명에 해당하는 것은?

> 중재절차에서 중재판정부는 당사자들의 지위를 보호하고 중재판정의 결과를 기다리는 동안 중재대상의 목적물의 처분이나 재산 도피 등을 제한하고 그 상태를 유지하도록 한다.

① 임시적 처분(interim measure)

② 최종판정(final award)

③ 자기심사권한(competence-competence)

④ 보수청구(remuneration)

68 무역보험에서 보험계약자나 피보험자에 의한 보험사고의 역선택을 방지하기 위한 내용으로 옳지 않은 것은?

① 보험기간의 제한

② 보험책임 시기(始期)의 제한

③ 포괄보험의 실시

④ 보험계약자의 통지의무

69 신용장거래에서 서류심사기준에 관한 설명으로 옳지 않은 것은?

① 상업송장상 물품의 기술은 신용장의 기술과 정확하게 일치하여야 한다.

② 신용장에서 별도의 언급이 없는 한, 운송서류의 원본은 유효기일 이내 그리고 선적일 후 21일 내에 제시되어야 한다.

③ 신용장에서 요구되지 않은 서류가 제시된 경우 은행은 이를 무시하고 제시인에게 반송할 수 있다.

④ 신용장 발행일자 이전에 발행된 서류는 그 제시일자보다 늦게 발행된 것일 수도 있다.

70 국제물품매매계약에 관한 협약(CISG)상 매도인의 계약위반에 따른 매수인의 구제권에 대한 설명으로 옳지 않은 것은?

① 대체물품인도청구권 – 물품이 계약과 불일치하고 그 불일치의 정도가 근본적 계약위반에 해당하는 경우에 매수인은 매도인에게 대체물품의 인도청구를 할 수 있다.

② 하자보완청구권 – 물품이 계약과 불일치하고 그 불일치의 정도가 근본적 계약위반에 해당되고 매수인이 모든 사정을 고려하여 자신에게 불리하지 않는 한 매도인에게 그 불일치의 보완을 청구할 수 있다.

③ 추가기간지정권 – 매수인은 매도인의 의무이행을 위하여 상당한 추가기간을 지정할 수 있는데 추가기간의 허용은 매수인의 의무가 아니라 재량에 따라 행사가 가능하다.

④ 계약해제권 – 매도인의 인도 불이행의 경우 근본적 계약위반이 아니더라도 매수인이 정한 최고기간 이내에 인도의 의무를 이행하지 않겠다는 의사를 명백히 한 경우에는 계약해제가 가능하다.

71 D/P, D/A 거래에 대한 설명으로 옳지 않은 것은?

① 수출상 입장에서는 D/P보다 D/A가 위험부담이 크다.

② D/P, D/A 거래가 신용장거래에 비하여 수입상에게 은행에 대한 비용부담이 적다.

③ D/P at sight뿐만 아니라 D/P usance도 있다.

④ D/P, D/A는 수출보험공사의 수출보험대상이 되지 않는다.

72 무역클레임에 대비하여 계약서에 삽입하는 조항에 관한 설명으로 옳지 않은 것은?

① Arbitration clause는 분쟁해결방법을 중재로 선택하는 경우에 사용하는 조항이다.

② Entire agreement clause는 계약서가 유일한 합의서이고, 다른 것의 내용은 인정하지 않는다는 완전합의 조항이다.

③ Non waiver clause는 클레임이나 권리의 포기는 서면으로 승인하거나 확인한 경우에만 포기한 것으로 간주한다는 조항이다.

④ Warranty Disclaimer clause는 통상적으로 요구되는 정도의 안정성 또는 기능 등에 대해 묵시적으로 보장하는 조항이다.

73 무역계약의 수량조건에 대한 설명으로 옳지 않은 것은?

① 중량의 단위는 ton, lb, kg 등이 있다.

② 영국식(long ton) 1ton의 무게는 1,024kg이다.

③ 순중량(net weight)은 포장무게 및 함유잡물의 무게를 공제한 순 상품 자체만의 무게이다.

④ 길이의 단위는 주로 생사(silk), 면사(cotton yearn), 인조견사(rayon)의 직물류 및 필름 등의 거래에 사용된다.

74 무역운송관련 헤이그-비스비 규칙상 운송인의 면책항목 중 나머지 셋과 가장 거리가 먼 것은?

① 포장이나 화인의 불충분성

② 해상의 인명이나 재산의 구조

③ 선장, 운송인의 사용인 등의 과실

④ 상당주의를 요하는 선박의 불내항성

75 두 국가가 외환위기대비나 무역결제를 지원하기 위해 자국 통화를 맡겨놓고 상대국 통화를 빌려오는 외환거래형태는?

① 통화선물(currency futures)

② 통화옵션(currency options)

③ 통화스왑(currency swap)

④ 팩토링(factoring)

<제1과목> 영문해석

01 In what circumstance does the following apply?

> Incoterms 2010 rules include the obligation to procure goods shipped as an alternative to the obligation to ship goods in the relevant Incoterms rules.

① deliver to the carrier
② deliver on board the vessel
③ sale of commodities sold during transit
④ arrange goods at seller's premises

02 Below is about demand guarantee which is internationally used. Which is wrong?

> A. Demand guarantee is a non-accessory obligation towards the beneficiary.
> B. The guarantor remains liable even if the obligation of the applicant is for any reason extinguished.
> C. The guarantor must pay on first demand with making objection or defence.
> D. URDG 758 is an international set of rules produced by ICC governing the rights and obligations of parties under demand guarantees.

① A only
② A + B only
③ C only
④ C + D only

03 What has a similar function with Demand guarantee?

| A. Surety Bond | B. Commercial L/C |
| C. Standby L/C | D. Aval |

① A only
② B only
③ C only
④ all of them

04 Which is NOT correct according to following situation?

> Goods are taken in charge at Daegu, Korea for transport to Long Beach, California, under a price term "CIP Long Beach, California, Incoterms 2010"

① The seller will arrange transportation.
② The seller will pay for freight to Long Beach.
③ Risk will pass to the buyer upon delivery of the goods to the carrier at Daegu.
④ The Buyer will take risk from the time the goods arrive at Long Beach

05 What does the following explain?

> This is nonnegotiable transport document and simply evidences that goods are on the way and should only be used when title and financing are not issues. Its function is contract, receipt, and invoice for the goods carried by sea.

① Charter party B/L
② Bill of Lading
③ Air waybill
④ Sea waybill

06 If seller and buyer enter into sales contract incorporating 'FCA Busan Container Depot', which of the following transport documents would be acceptable to the buyer?

A. Air Waybill marked 'freight paid at destination'.
B. Bill of Lading marked freight paid.
C. Combined Bill of lading marked freight payable at destination.
D. Multimodal Bill of lading marked freight paid.

① A
② A + B
③ C
④ C + D

07 Incoterms are a series of pre-defined commercial terms published by the International Chamber of Commerce (ICC) relating to international trade rules. What is WRONG in the explanation of Incoterms 2010?

① Incoterms by themselves do not define where title transfers.
② Incoterms support the sales contract by defining the respective obligations, costs and risks involved in the delivery of goods from the Seller to the Buyer.
③ Incoterms are used in the Sales Contract, suitable INCOTERM rule and place or port are to be specified.
④ DDP and DAP are the Incoterms where the Seller has responsibility for import.

08 Below explains Bill of Exchange. Who is the underlined one?

A bill of exchange is an unconditional order, in writing addressed by <u>one</u> person to another, signed by the person giving it, requesting the person to whom it is addressed to pay certain amount at sight or at a fixed date.

① drawer
② drawee
③ payee
④ payer

09 What is NOT watching point in application of Incoterms 2010?

① DDP : Some taxes such as VAT are only payable by a locally-registered business entity, so there may be no mechanism for the seller to make payment.
② CPT : The buyer should enquire whether the CPT price includes THC, so as to avoid disputes after arrival of goods.
③ EXW : Although the seller is not obliged to load the goods, if the seller does so, it is recommended to do at the buyer's risk.
④ FOB : If the goods are in containers, FOB may be appropriate.

10 What is most WRONG in the explanation of global business ?

① Protectionism holds that regulation of international trade is important to ensure the markets protection.
② Tariffs, subsidies and quotas are common examples of protectionism.
③ FDI leads to a growth in the gross domestic product of investing country.
④ As a result of international trade, the market becomes more competitive by bringing a cheaper product to the consumer.

[11~12] Read the following and answer the questions.

I recently purchased from your catalog OEM Toner Cartridge No. 123 for USD 74.99 per piece, which was advertised to be 20 percent below the normal price. I received the toner cartridge two days later and felt completely satisfied with my purchase.

While looking through the Sunday edition of THE BOSTON GLOBE yesterday, I noticed the same toner cartridge selling for USD64.99 at Global Computer Outlet.

You say you won't be undersold on any merchandise. If that's true, I'd appreciate a refund of USD (   ) since we bought 100,000 cartridges. Thank you.

Sincerely, Skip
Simmons

11 What is MOST suitable for the blank?

① 10

② 1,000,000

③ 100,000

④ 6,499,000

12 Which is MOST likely to be enclosed in this letter?

① writer's first inquiry letter

② a copy of invoice and Global Computer Outlet's advertisement

③ a copy of catalog

④ a copy of price list which Simmons sent

[13~14] Read the following and answer the questions.

I read your ad in the January issue of Mobile Homes Monthly looking for Carefree Mobile Homes in the Atlanta area.

I would like to learn more about Carefree Mobile Homes and their incentive program for dealers. Mobile Homes are very popular in this area, and I am most interested in hearing more about your products and marketing opportunities.

13 What is being sought in Mobile Homes Monthly?

① job offer for technician

② retail dealership

③ customer recruitment for Mobile Homes service

④ promotion to offer special discount

14 Who is the receiver of the letter?

① magazine editor

② dealer in Atlanta

③ Carefree Mobile Homes company

④ customer center for mobile service

[15~17] Read the following letter and answer the questions.

I have now received our (A) assessor's report with reference to your claim in which you asked for (B) compensation for damage to two turbine engines which were shipped ex-Liverpool on the Freemont on 11 October, for delivery to your customer, D.V. Industries, Hamburg.

The report states that the B/L was claused by the captain of the vessel, with a (C) comment on cracks in the casing of the machinery.

Our assessor believes that these cracks were the first signs of the weakening and splitting of the casing during the (D) voyage, and that this eventually damaged the turbines themselves.

(　　) I am sorry that we cannot help you further.

15 Which could NOT be replaced with the underlined (A), (B), (C) and (D) parts?

① A : surveyor

② B : compliment

③ C : remark

④ D : trip

16 Which could not be replaced with the underlined claused?

① commentary

② dirty

③ unclean

④ foul

17 Which of the following BEST fits the blank in the letter?

① I regret that we can accept liability for goods if they are shipped clean.

② I regret that we cannot accept liability for goods unless they are shipped clean.

③ I am very happy that we accept liability for goods as they are shipped clean.

④ I regret that we cannot accept liability for goods even though they are shipped clean.

18 Under UCP 600, what is NOT correct?

- Seller is in Seoul, Korea
- Buyer is in Frankfurt, Germany
- Seller sells USD 100,000.00 worth of goods to Buyer Buyer uses Deutche Bank to open the Letter of Credit
- This unconfirmed letter of credit requires a '90 days after sight' draft from the beneficiary.

① The drawer of draft is seller.

② Issuing bank is to reimburse for complying presentation, whether or not the nominated bank purchased before the maturity of draft.

③ The draft shall be drawn on the buyer.

④ The seller may apply silent confirmation.

19 What kind of charter does the following explain?

It is a charter, an arrangement for the hiring of a vessel, whereby no administration or technical maintenance is included as part of the agreement. In this case, the charterer obtains possession and full control of the vessel along with the legal and financial responsibility for it. Also the charterer pays for all operating expenses, including fuel, crew, port expenses and P&I and hull insurance.

① Demise charter

② Voyage charter

③ Time charter

④ Trip charter

20 **What is the MAIN purpose of the letter?**

> Dear Mr. Colson :
>
> Thank you for your application for credit at Barrow. We appreciate your interest.
>
> Your personal references are exceptionally good, and your record of hard work indicates that your business prospects are good for the near future.
>
> Unfortunately, at the present, your financial condition only partially meets Barrow's requirements. We cannot extend the USD 500,000 open credit you requested.
>
> Please call me at your convenience. I am sure we can set up a program of gradually increasing credit that will benefit both of us. Meanwhile, remember that deliveries on cash purchase are made within two days.
>
> Let me hear from you soon. We are interested in your business venture.

① to praise the good credit report

② to offer the credit increase

③ to deny credit extension

④ to continue the business with the company

21 **Which is NOT correct in accordance with CISG?**

① An offer becomes effective when it reaches the offeree.

② An offer, even if it is irrevocable, may be withdrawn if the withdrawal reaches the offeree before or at the same time as the offer.

③ A statement made by or other conduct of the offeree indicating assent to an offer is an acceptance.

④ Silence or inactivity in itself amounts to acceptance.

22 **Which of the following is NOT covered by ICC(C)?**

① explosion

② washing overboard

③ jettison

④ general average sacrifice

23 **What is WRONG with the roles of freight forwarders?**

① They act as an agent on behalf of shipper in moving the cargo to the destination.

② They are familiar with the methods of shipment and required documents relating to foreign trade.

③ They have primary responsibility for paying duties and taxes for import customs charges.

④ They assist the customers in preparing price quotations by advising on freight costs, port charges, cost of documentation, handling fee, etc.

24 **Under UCP 600, what is NOT an appropriate statement for the amendments of Letter of Credit?**

① A credit can neither be amended nor cancelled without the agreement of Seller, Buyer and issuing bank.

② The terms and conditions of the original credit will remain in force for Seller until Seller communicates its acceptance of the amendment.

③ If Seller fails to give notification of acceptance or rejection of an amendment, a presentation that complies with any not yet accepted amendment will be deemed to be notification of acceptance of such amendment.

④ Partial acceptance of an amendment is not allowed and will be deemed to be notification of rejection of the amendment.

25 **The following statement is a part of contract. What kind of clause is it?**

> If any provision of this Agreement is subsequently held invalid or unenforceable by any court or authority agent, such invalidity or unenforceability shall in no way affect the validity or enforceability of any other provisions thereof.

① Non-waiver clause

② Infringement clause

③ Assignment clause

④ Severability clause

<제2과목> 영작문

26 Which of the following BEST fits the blank?

In the event of (   ), the assured may claim from any underwriters concerned, but he is not entitled to recover more than the statutory indemnity.

① reinsurance
② double insurance
③ coinsurance
④ full insurance

27 Which of the following statements has a different purpose?

① We would advise you to proceed with caution in your dealings with the firm in question.
② We regret that we have to give you unfavorable information about that firm.
③ According to our records, they have never failed to meet our bills since they opened an account with us.
④ You would run some risk entering into a credit transaction with that company.

28 Which of the following BEST completes the blanks in the letter?

We would like to send (A)-Heathrow (B) Riyadh, Saudi Arabia, 12 crates of assorted glassware, to be delivered (C) the next 10 days.

① A : ex, B : to, C : within
② A : ex, B : to, C : in
③ A : from, B : through, C : within
④ A : from, B : through, C : in

29 Which is the proper Incoterms 2010 term for the following?

The seller delivers the goods on board the vessel nominated by the buyer at the named port of shipment or procures the goods already so delivered. The risk of loss of or damage to the goods passes when the goods are on board the vessel, and the buyer bears all costs from that moment onwards.

① FAS
② FCA
③ FOB
④ CFR

30 The following is related to insurance. What are the proper words to be filled in the blanks A and B?

In order to recover under this insurance, the (A) must have an insurable interest in the subject-matter insured at the time of (B).

① A : assurer, B : the loss
② A : assured, B : the loss
③ A : assurer, B : the insurance contract
④ A : assured, B : the insurance contract

31 Put the right words in the blanks.

> [Complaint]
>
> I strongly object to the extra charge of USD 9,000 which you have added to my statement. When I sent my cheque for USD 256,000 last week, I thought it cleared this balance.
>
> [Answer]
>
> We received your letter today complaining of an extra charge of USD 9,000 on your May statement. I think if you check the statement you will find that the amount (A) was USD 265,000 not USD 256,000 which accounts for the USD 9,000 (B).

① A : due, B : difference
② A : for, B : price
③ A : of, B : charges
④ A : received, B : less

32 Choose the right word(s) for the blank below.

> (   ) in international trade is a sale where the goods are shipped and delivered before payment is due, which is typically in 30, 60 or 90 days.
>
> Obviously, this option is advantageous to the importer in terms of cash flow and cost, but it is consequently a risky option for an exporter.

① A COD transaction
② A CAD transaction
③ An open account transaction
④ A D/P transaction

[33 ~ 34] Read the following and answer.

> While we cannot give you an explanation at present, we are looking into the problem and will contact you again shortly.
>
> As we are sending out orders promptly, I think these delays may be occurring during (   ). I shall get in touch with the haulage contractors. Would you please return samples of the items you are dissatisfied with, and then I will send them to our factory in Daejon for tests.

33 What is the main purpose of the letter above?

① To give complaints in the soonest manner
② To ask for more time to investigate the complaint
③ To investigate the delay with carrier
④ To return samples damaged

34 What is best for the blank?

① investigation
② transit
③ arrival
④ dispatch

35 Which is MOST appropriate for the blank?

> I was surprised and sorry to hear that your Order No.1555 had not reached you. On enquiry I found that it had been delayed by a local dispute on the cargo vessel SS Arirang on which it had been loaded. I am now trying to get the goods transferred to the SS Samoa which is scheduled to sail for Yokohama before the end of next week.
> (   ).

① I shall remind you if this happens again
② Please keep me be informed of the sailings
③ We can reach an amicable agreement in the near future
④ I shall keep you informed of the progress

[36～37] Which of the pairs does NOT have the similar intention?

36 ① Can you give me some cost estimates on that?
→ I was wondering roughly how much your service would cost.
② I am not convinced that acting on this plan is in the best interests of my team.
→ I am behind this plan 100%.
③ We appreciate your asking us and are willing to comply with your request.
→ Thank you very much for asking. Let me give you a hand, please.
④ We have been forced to withdraw ourselves from this project.
→ We have no choice but to pull ourselves out of the project.

37 ① The contents of the meeting should be kept strictly confidential.
→ Please keep the things discussed in the meeting to yourself.
② I am not completely against your thoughts.
→ I give my conditional support to your proposal.
③ I am wondering whether you could let me put off the deadline.
→ I would be grateful if you could grant me an extension of the original deadline.
④ The pleasure of your company is requested when we visit them.
→ We hope that all the people in your firm will be very satisfied at this.

[38～39] Read the following and answer the questions.

Dear Mrs Johnson
Thank you for your letter inquiring for electric heaters. I am pleased to enclose (a) a copy of our latest illustrated catalogue.
You may be particularly interested in our newest heater, the FX21 model. Without any increase in fuel consumption, it gives out 15% (b) more heat than earlier models. You will find (c) details of our terms in the price list printed on the inside front cover of the catalogue.
Perhaps you would consider (　　) to (d) provide you of an opportunity to test its efficiency. At the same time this would enable you to see for yourself the high quality of material.
If you have any questions, please contact me on 6234917.

38 Which is MOST suitable for the blank?
① taking an order
② placing a volume order
③ placing a trial order
④ to place an initial order

39 Which of the following is grammatically INCORRECT?
① (a)　　　② (b)　　　③ (c)　　　④ (d)

40 Fill in the blank with the BEST word(s).

A written one to pay a determinate sum of money made between two parties is a (　　). The party who promises to pay is called the maker; the party who is to be paid is the payee.

① promissory note
② letter of credit
③ draft
④ Bill of Exchange

41 Which is NOT a good match?

> An insurance document, such as (A), (B) or (C) under an open cover, must appear to be issued and signed by an insurance company, an underwriter or their agents or their (D).

① (A) cover note
② (B) insurance policy
③ (C) insurance certificate
④ (D) proxies

42 Which is INCORRECT under UCP 600?

① The words "from" and "after" when used to determine a maturity date include the date mentioned.
② Banks deal with documents and not with goods, services or performance to which the documents may relate.
③ Branches of a bank in different countries are considered to be separate banks.
④ Applicant means the party on whose request the credit is issued.

43 Choose the INCORRECT one about arbitration.

① Arbitration decisions are final and binding on the both parties.
② Disputes are resolved more quickly by arbitration than by litigation, saving time and cost.
③ Both parties may choose the arbitrators, place, language.
④ Proceedings are open to the public and the arbitral award is disclosed.

44 What does Blank refer to?

> (   ) literally means "as it arrives". It is used in contract for shipment of grain in bulk to signify that the consignor will accept the goods in whatever condition they arrive, so long as they were in good order at time of shipment, as evidenced by a certificate of quality issued by an impartial inspection agency.

① GMQ
② Tale Quale
③ Rye Term
④ Sea Damaged Term

45 Which is NOT a replacement for the underlined?

① We shall be compelled to place the matter in the hands of our lawyer.
(institute legal proceeding for the matter)
② We have to inform you that it is not yet possible for us to meet our obligations.
(fulfill our commitments)
③ Thank you for writing to us so frankly about your inability to pay your debt.
(competence to meet your debt)
④ There have, however, been several instances in the past when you have asked for extra time to settle your account.
(balance your account)

46 Choose a correct one in O/A payment.

① It is dangerous to use when the importer has favorable payment history.
② It is safe to use if the freight forwarder has been deemed to be creditworthy in order for the trade transaction.
③ O/A is the most advantageous option to the importer in terms of cash flow and cost, but it is consequently the highest risky option for an exporter.
④ O/A means Opening Applicant.

47 What is THIS?

> THIS is the term used to describe the offence of trying to conceal money that has been obtained through offences such as drugs trafficking.
>
> In other words, money obtained from certain crimes, such as extortion, insider trading, drug trafficking and illegal gambling is 'dirty'.

① money laundering
② fraud
③ illegal investment
④ abnormal remittance

48 According to the letter, what would be MOST suitable for the blank in common?

> We certainly appreciate your interest in Maxoine Sportswear. Nevertheless, I am afraid we cannot give you the information you requested.
>
> Because we do not sell our garments directly to the consumer, we try to keep _____ between ourselves and our dealers. It is our way of meriting both the loyalty and good faith of those with whom we do business. Clearly, divulging _____ to a consumer would be a violation of a trust.

① our dealer lists
② our wholesale prices
③ the highest price
④ our consumers' information

49 Which is most AWKWARD English writing?

① 우리 소프트웨어 제품에 관심을 보여주신 귀사의 4월 8일자 문의에 대해 감사드립니다.
   → Thank you for your inquiry on April 8, expressing interest in our software products.

② 오늘 주문서 No.9087에 대한 배송을 받고 포장을 풀었을 때, 우리는 전 품목이 완전히 파손되었음을 발견했습니다.
   → Today we received delivery of our order No.9087, and unpacked, we found all items were completely damaging.

③ 신용장의 잔액은 미화 15,000달러이므로 그 범위 내에서 선적해 주십시오.
   → As the balance of L/C is USD15,000, please make shipment within the amount.

④ 귀사가 신용장의 유효 기간 내에 주문을 이행하지 않았으므로 당사는 신용장을 취소하겠습니다.
   → As you have not executed the order within the validity of L/C, we will make cancellation of the L/C.

50 Which is NOT grammatically correct?

① 귀하가 겪은 불편에 대해 깊이 사과드립니다.
   → We deeply apologize for the inconvenience you have experienced.

② 2월 20일까지 귀사 부담으로 XT-4879 케이블 모뎀 500개를 항공 화물편으로 보내주시기 바랍니다.
   → Please send us 500 XT-4879 cable modems by February 20 by air freight at your expense.

③ 귀사의 8월 5일자 주문서에 대한 신용장이 개설되도록 귀사 거래 은행에 신용장 개설을 촉구하여 주십시오.
   → Please arrange with your bank to open a letter of credit for your order of August 5.

④ 귀사가 주문하신 Model No.289E 재봉틀이 단종되었음을 알려드리게 되어 유감입니다.
   → We are sorry to inform you of the sewing machine(Model No.289E) you ordered have discontinued.

\<제3과목\> 무역실무

51 아래 글상자는 무역계약에서 국제상관습의 의의에 관한 설명이다. 공란에 들어갈 내용을 바르게 연결한 것은?

> (ⓐ)의 (ⓑ)은 극히 간결한 형태로 표현되고 있음에도 불구하고, 대량의 무역거래가 신속 안전하게 이행되는 것은 수백 년에 걸쳐서 형성된 (ⓒ)이란 형태의 (ⓓ)에 의하여 (ⓐ)을 보완하여 왔기 때문이다.

① ⓐ 국제상관습   ⓑ 명시조항
　 ⓒ 무역계약   ⓓ 묵시조항

② ⓐ 국제상관습   ⓑ 묵시조항
　 ⓒ 무역계약   ⓓ 명시조항

③ ⓐ 무역계약   ⓑ 묵시조항
　 ⓒ 국제상관습   ⓓ 명시조항

④ ⓐ 무역계약   ⓑ 명시조항
　 ⓒ 국제상관습   ⓓ 묵시조항

52 해상보험에서 사용하는 용어에 대한 설명으로 옳지 않은 것은?

① 손인은 손해의 원인으로 좌초, 충돌, 화재 등을 들 수 있다.

② 위험은 손해발생가능성을 말하는 것으로 반드시 손해로 연결되는 것을 말한다.

③ 위태는 손해발생의 가능성을 증가시키는 상태를 말한다.

④ 보험금액은 보험사고 발생 시 보험자가 보상하는 최고한도가 된다.

53 결제방식에 대한 설명으로 옳지 않은 것은?

① 대금회수와 관련하여 신용장은 안전하지만 국제팩토링은 다소 위험하다.

② 신용장에서는 환어음네고로 결제가 이루어지고 국제팩토링의 경우 전도금융이 이루어진다.

③ 신용장은 일람불환어음이나 기한부환어음을 요구하지만 국제팩토링은 환어음을 요구하지 않는다.

④ 신용장과 추심결제에서 사용되는 서류는 환어음과 선적서류이다.

54 양도된 신용장의 최종적인 지급의무를 지는 당사자로 옳은 것은?

① 제1수익자
② 신용장 양도은행
③ 개설의뢰인
④ 원신용장 개설은행

55 보험관련 설명 중 옳지 않은 것은?

① 화물보험의 보험기간은 장소로 표시한다.

② 해상보험에서 부보되는 위험은 Warehouse to warehouse Clause에 의한 해륙혼합위험이다.

③ 소급약관이나 포괄예정보험은 보험계약기간과 보험기간이 일치하게 된다.

④ 전쟁위험의 보험기간은 화물이 육상에 있는 동안에는 해당되지 않는다.

56 컨테이너와 관련된 설명으로 옳지 않은 것은?

① 컨테이너선의 대형화는 항구에서의 하역작업에 많은 시간을 요하는 한계성이 있다.

② 컨테이너의 한계성은 컨테이너에 적입하는데 한계상품이나 부적합상품이 있다는 것이다.

③ LCL화물들은 CFS에 반입되어 FCL화물로 혼재되어 목적지별로 분류된다.

④ 컨테이너의 사용으로 포장비용을 줄일 수 있고 선박의 정박일수도 단축할 수 있다.

57 추정전손에 대한 설명으로 옳지 않은 것은?

① Constructive Total Loss이라고 하고 해석전손이라고도 한다.

② 화물손해 발행 시, 손상을 수선하는 비용과 화물을 그 목적항까지 운송하는 비용을 합산한 비용이 도착 시의 화물 가액을 초과할 것으로 예상되는 경우가 추정전손에 포함된다.

③ 추정전손이 있을 경우에는 피보험자는 그 손해를 분손으로 처리할 수도 있고 보험자에게 보험목적물을 위부하고 그 손해를 현실전손에 준하여 처리할 수도 있다.

④ 선박이 행방불명되고 상당한 기간 경과 후까지 그 소식을 모를 경우는 추정전손으로 처리될 수 있다.

58 적하보험에 대한 설명으로 옳지 않은 것은?

① 객관적 위험이 이미 발생했거나 위험이 없는 경우, 보험계약당사자가 이 사실을 모르는 경우에는 보험계약 체결이 가능한데 이러한 보험을 소급보험이라고 한다.

② 보험금액이 보험가액보다 적은 경우의 보험은 일부보험(under insurance)이다.

③ Premium은 보험자의 위험부담에 대한 대가로서 피보험자나 보험계약자가 보험자에게 지급하는 금전이다.

④ 피보험자는 보험계약이 체결될 때 보험목적물에 이해관계를 가져야 하나 손해 발생 시에는 보험목적물에 이해관계를 가질 필요는 없다.

59 아래 글상자 내용은 어떤 원칙에 관한 것인가?

- UN국제물품복합운송조약에서 채택한 원칙
- 손해발생구간의 확인여부에 관계없이 동일한 책임원칙을 적용하지만, 손해발생구간이 확인되어 그 구간에 적용될 법에 의한 책임한도액이 UN국제물품복합운송조약에서의 금액보다 높을 경우 높은 한도액을 적용한다는 원칙
- 운송도중 발생한 물품의 멸실이나 손상에 대한 손해배상액은 손해발생구간이 판명되면 구간의 단일운송협약상 책임한도액이 적용되며, 손해발생구간이 불명일 때는 일반원칙이 적용되도록 함

① Network Liability System
② Uniform Liability System
③ Modified Uniform Liability System
④ Liability for Negligence

60 Incoterms 2010에 대한 설명으로 옳은 것은?

① 매도인과 매수인 간에 강제적으로 적용되는 국제규칙이다.

② 국제매매계약뿐만 아니라 국내매매계약에도 사용가능하다.

③ 당사자 간에 합의되었더라도, 전자적 형태의 통신은 종이에 의한 통신과는 다른 효력이 부여된다.

④ 물품소유권의 이전 및 계약위반의 효과를 매도인, 매수인 입장에서 각각 다루고 있다.

61 양도가능신용장에 대한 설명으로 옳지 않은 것을 모두 고르면?

ㄱ 중계무역은 양도가능 신용장이 발행되는 경우에만 가능하다.

ㄴ 제2의 수익자가 1개 회사인 경우, L/C금액의 전부를 양도하는 전액양도만 허용된다.

ㄷ 제1의 수익자는 복수의 제2수익자에게, 분할양도할 수 있다.

ㄹ 제2의 수익자가 제3의 수익자에게 양도하는 경우 개설의뢰인과 개설은행 모두에게 사전 양해를 얻는다면 가능하다.

ㅁ 국내 소재 제2의 수익자에게도 양도하는 경우 Local L/C라고 한다.

① ㄱ, ㄴ, ㄷ, ㄹ
② ㄱ, ㄴ, ㄷ, ㅁ
③ ㄱ, ㄴ, ㄹ, ㅁ
④ ㄴ, ㄷ, ㄹ, ㅁ

62 B/L상에 "Shipper's Load & Count"와 같은 문구가 있는 경우, 이에 대한 설명으로 옳지 않은 것은?

① Liner를 이용한 운송이다.
② Container 운송이다.
③ 하역비는 FIO 조건이 적용된다.
④ B/L의 발행일자 외에 선적일자가 별도로 기재되어야 한다.

63 청약 등에 대한 내용 설명으로 옳지 않은 것은?

① 주문서도 청약으로 볼 수 있으나 확인(Confirmation)이나 승인(Acknowledgement)이 있어야 계약이 성립된다.

② 청약조건을 실질적으로 변동시키는 것은 대금지급 변경, 분쟁해결 변경, 인도조건의 조회 등이다.

③ Cross offer는 동일한 조건으로 매도청약과 매수청약이 동시에 이루어지는 것으로 영미법에서는 계약이 성립되지 않는다.

④ 조건부청약은 청약자의 최종확인이 있어야 계약이 성립되며 서브콘 오퍼라고도 한다.

64 Frustration에 대한 설명으로 옳은 것은?

① Frustration의 성립요건은 계약목적물의 물리적 멸실, 후발적 위법 등이며 계약목적물의 상업적 멸실은 해당되지 않는다.

② Frustration은 신의성실의 원칙에서의 사정변경의 원칙과 관련이 있다.

③ 주요공급원의 예기치 못한 폐쇄는 Frustration에 해당되지만 농작물의 흉작, 불작황은 해당되지 않는다.

④ Frustration의 성립은 즉각 소급하여 계약을 소멸시키고 양당사자의 의무를 면제한다.

65 신협회적하약관 ICC(B) 조건에서 보상하는 손해로 옳지 않은 것은?

① 쌍방과실충돌

② 공동해손·구조비

③ 약관상 면책사항 이외의 우연적 사고에 의한 손해

④ 본선·부선에의 선적 또는 양륙작업 중 바다에 떨어지거나 갑판에 추락하여 발생한 포장단위당의 전손

66 복합운송증권의 특징에 대한 설명으로 옳지 않은 것은?

① 화물의 멸실, 손상에 대한 전 운송구간을 커버하는 일관책임을 진다.

② 선하증권과 달리 운송인뿐만 아니라 운송주선인에 의해서도 발행된다.

③ 화물이 본선적재 전에 복합운송인이 수탁 또는 수취한 상태에서 발행된다.

④ 지시식으로 발행된 경우 백지배서에 의해서만 양도가 가능하다.

67 포페이팅에 대한 설명 중 옳지 않는 것은?

① 환어음 또는 약속어음 등 유통가능한 증서를 상환청구권 없이(Without Recourse) 매입하는 방식이다.

② 포페이팅은 신용장 또는 보증(Aval) 방식으로 이루어지며 어음에 대한 할인은 보통 수출상이 최종적으로 부담한다.

③ 기계, 중장비, 산업설비, 건설장비 등 연불조건 구매가 이루어지는 경우 중요한 결제수단이다.

④ 포페이팅의 가장 큰 장점은 연불조건 구매와 같이 중장기 거래에 따른 신용위험(Credit risk) 등을 회피할 수 있다는 것이다.

68 해상보험에서 위험에 대한 설명으로 옳지 않은 것은?

① Perils of the Seas는 해상고유의 위험으로 Stranding, Sinking, Collision, Heavy Wheather를 포함한다.

② Perils on the Seas는 해상위험으로 Fire, Jettison, Barratry, Pirates, Rovers, Thieves를 포함한다.

③ 포괄담보 방식에서는 보험자가 면책위험을 제외한 모든 손해를 담보하는데, ICC(A) 또는 W/A가 여기에 속한다.

④ 갑판적, 환적, 강제하역, 포장불충분 등 위험이 변경되는 경우 보험자는 원칙적으로 변경 후 사고에 대해 면책된다.

69 해상보험의 보상원칙으로 옳지 않은 것은?

① 보험사고가 발생하더라도 보험금액을 보상하는 것이 아니라 피보험자의 실손해만을 보상하는 실손보상원칙을 따른다.

② 적하보험은 기평가보험으로서 통상 CIF 가액의 110%로 보험금액이 결정된다.

③ 보험자는 피보험자에게 보험금을 지급하면 피보험목적물에 대한 권리를 이전받는 대위원칙을 따른다.

④ 보험자는 피보험자가 입은 직접적인 손해뿐만 아니라 간접 손해도 보상하는 손해보상원칙을 따른다.

70 선하증권에 대한 설명으로 옳지 않은 것은?

① 운송계약의 추정적 증거(Prima facie evidence)이다.

② 운송인이 물품을 수취했다는 물품의 수령증이다.

③ 'Said by shipper to contain'과 같은 부지약관이 있어도 신용장 거래에서 수리된다.

④ 권리증권으로 유통이 가능하며 'Consignee'란에 수화인이 기재되어 유통될 수 있다.

71 Incoterms 2010상 FOB 규칙에 대한 설명으로 옳지 않은 것은?

① 매도인이 선적항에서 매수인이 지정한 본선에 수출통관된 계약상품을 선적하면 매도인의 물품인도 의무가 완료된다.

② FCA 조건에 매도인의 본선으로의 선적의무가 추가된 조건이다.

③ 매수인은 자기의 책임과 비용부담 하에 운송계약을 체결하고 선박명, 선적기일 등을 매도인에게 통지해 주어야 한다.

④ 컨테이너 운송에서 매도인이 물품을 갑판이 아닌 CY 등 다른 장소에 인도하는 경우에는 FOB 대신 FCA 조건을 사용해야 한다.

72 계약서에 들어가는 선적조건에 대한 설명으로 옳지 않은 것은?

① 신용장상에 할부선적 횟수가 규정되었을 때는 어느 한 부분이라도 선적이 이행되지 않았다면 그 선적분과 모든 잔여 선적분은 무효가 된다.

② 선적일은 수취선하증권이 발행된 경우에는 발행일이 곧 선적일이다.

③ 'on or about'에 대한 선적 시기에 대한 해석은 선적이 지정일자로부터 양끝의 일자를 포함하여 5일 전후까지의 기간 내에 선적되어야 한다.

④ 천재지변, 전쟁 등 불가항력에 의한 선적지연의 경우 원칙적으로 매도인은 면책된다.

73 화물손해에 대한 해상운송인의 면책 사유로 옳지 않은 것은?

① 운송인은 항해 중 선장, 선원의 행위, 태만 또는 과실로 인하여 발생한 화물의 손해는 면책된다.

② 포장의 불충분성으로 인하여 발생하는 멸실이나 손상은 면책된다.

③ 선박의 화재로 인하여 발생한 화물의 손해는 면책되나 운송인의 고의로 인한 것이 아니어야 한다.

④ 운송인은 침몰, 좌초와 통상적인 풍파로 인하여 발생한 화물의 멸실이나 손상은 면책된다.

74 환어음의 필수기재사항에 해당되는 것만으로 옳게 나열된 것은?

① 지급인, 지급기일, 수취인, 발행일 및 발행지

② 환어음표시문자, 지급인, 지급지, 신용장 번호

③ 금액, 지급지, 어음번호, 발행인의 서명

④ 상환불능문언, 환어음표시문자, 발행인의 서명, 환율문언

75 CISG상 유효한 승낙으로 간주되는 것은?

① 침묵에 의한 승낙

② 청약에 대해 동의의 의사를 표시하는 피청약자의 행위

③ 무행위(Inactivity)에 의한 승낙

④ 동일한 거래조건을 담은 교차 청약(Cross offer)

<제1과목> 영문해석

01 Choose WRONG part of L/C explanation.

> The letter of credit is probably the most widely used method of financing for both (A) export and import shipments.
>
> In establishing a letter of credit, the buyer applies to his own bank for a specified amount (B) in favor of the buyer. The buyer stipulates the (C) documents which the seller must present, the duration of the credit, (D) the tenor of drafts which may be drawn, on whom they may be drawn, when shipments are to be made, and all other particulars in the transaction.

① (A)　　② (B)　　③ (C)　　④ (D)

[02 ~ 03] Read the following and answer.

> Dear Mr. Cox
>
> We are a large motorcycle wholesale chain with outlets throughout Korea, and are interested in the heavy touring bikes displayed on your stand at the Tokyo Trade Fair recently.
>
> There is an increasing demand here for this type of machine. Sales of larger machines have increased by more than 70% in the last two years, especially to the 40~50 age group, which wants more powerful bikes and can afford them.
>
> We are looking for a supplier who will offer us an exclusive agency to introduce heavy machines. At present we represent a number of manufacturers, but only sell machines up to 600cc, which would not compete with your 750cc, 1000cc, and 1200cc models.
>
> We operate on a 10% commission basis on net list prices, with an additional 3% del credere commission if required, and we estimate you could expect an annual turnover in excess of US $5,000,000.00 With an advertising allowance we could probably double this figure.
>
> We look forward to hearing from you.
>
> Steve Kim

02 What can NOT be inferred?

① Steve would like to represent same line of bikes with their current suppliers.

② Mr. Cox's company is engaged in heavy touring bikes.

③ Steve Kim may take end-buyers' credit risk.

④ 40~50 age Korean consumers tend to buy bikes with large engine displacement.

03 Which is NOT related with del credere?

① Del credere agent here guarantees that a buyer is trustworthy.

② Del credere agent here compensates the principal in case the buyer defaults.

③ To cover credit risk, del credere agents charge higher commission rates.

④ A del credere agent is an agent who guarantees the solvency of third parties with whom the agent contracts on behalf of the buyer.

04 What could mostly represent the underlying transaction?

> The terms of a credit are independent of the underlying transaction even if a credit expressly refers to that transaction. To avoid unnecessary costs, delays, and disputes in the examination of documents, however, the applicant and beneficiary should carefully consider which documents should be required, by whom they should be produced and the time frame for presentation.

① sales contract

② carriage contract

③ proforma invoice

④ certificate of origin

05 The following is about DAT under Incoterms 2010. Choose the wrong part.

> The seller delivers when the goods, (a) once unloaded from the arriving means of transport, are placed at the disposal of (b) the buyer at a named terminal at the named port or place of destination. "Terminal" (c) includes any place, whether covered or not, such as a quay, warehouse, container yard or road, rail or air cargo terminal. (d) If the parties intend the buyer to bear the risks and costs involved in transporting and handling the goods from the terminal to another place, then the DAP or DDP rules should be used.

① (a)　　② (b)　　③ (c)　　④ (d)

06 Choose the LEAST correct translation.

> (1) If a credit is transferred to more than one second beneficiary, (2) rejection of an amendment by one or more second beneficiary does not invalidate the acceptance by any other second beneficiary, (3) with respect to which the transferred credit will be amended accordingly. (4) For any second beneficiary that rejected the amendment, the transferred credit will remain unamended.

① 신용장이 하나 이상의 제2수익자에게 양도된 경우에는

② 하나 또는 그 이상의 제2수익자에 의한 조건변경의 거절은 어떤 다른 제2수익자에 의한 승낙을 무효로 하지 아니하고

③ 따라서 승낙한 제2수익자와 관련하여 양도된 신용장은 조건변경이 되고

④ 조건변경을 거절한 제2수익자에 대하여는, 양도된 신용장은 조건변경 없이 유지된다.

07 Which is NOT correct according to the letter?

> Dear Mr. Richardson
>
> We were pleased to receive your order of 15 April for a further supply of CD players.
> However, owing to current difficult conditions, we have to ensure that our many customers keep their accounts within reasonable limits. Only in this way we can meet our own commitments.
> At present the balance of your account stands at over US$1,800.00 We hope that you will be able to reduce it before we grant credit for further supplies.
> In the circumstances we should be grateful if you would send us your check for half the amount owed. We could then arrange to supply the goods now requested and charge them to your account.

① The writer is a seller.
② This is not the first time that the writer has business with Mr. Richardson.
③ The writer asks the receiver to send the check for current order.
④ This is a reply to the order.

[08~09] Read the following and answer the questions.

> We must express surprise that the firm mentioned in your enquiry of 25th May have given our name as a reference.
> As far as we know, they are a reputable firm, but we have no certain knowledge of their financial position. It is true that they have placed orders with us on a number of occasions during the past two years, but the amounts involved have been small compared with the sum mentioned in your letter; and even so, accounts were not always settled on time.
> _____. We accept your assurance that the information we give will be treated in strict confidence and regret that we cannot be more helpful.

08 According to the context, which is the best sentence in the blank?

① Therefore, we find this company to be a good credit rating.
② This, we feel, is a case in which caution is necessary and suggest that you make additional enquiries through an agency.
③ Our company was established in 1970 and has been enjoying steady growth in its business with excellent sales.
④ We regret that the amount of obligations you now carry makes it difficult for us to agree to allow you credit terms.

09 The passage in the box is a reply to the letter. Which of the following is LEAST to be included in the previous letter?

① Their requirements may amount to approximately US$200,000.00 a quarter and we should be grateful for your opinion of their ability to meet commitments of this size.
② They state that they have regularly traded with you over the past two years and have given us your name as a reference.
③ We should appreciate it if you would kindly tell us in confidence whether you have found this company to be thoroughly reliable in their dealings with you and prompt in settling their accounts.
④ We would appreciate a prompt decision concerning our order once you have contacted our references.

10 Which can NOT be inferred from the following correspondence?

> Dear Mr. Han,
>
> With reference to your letter, we are pleased to inform you that we have been able to secure the vessel you asked for.
> She is the SS Eagle and is docked at present in Busan. She is a bulk carrier with a cargo capacity of seven thousand tons, and has a speed of 24 knots which will certainly be able to make the number of trips in two months.
> Once the charter is confirmed, we will send you a charter party.
>
> Yours sincerely

① Shipper has a lot of goods in containers.
② Time charter is appropriate for the transaction.
③ The charter party to be issued is not negotiable.
④ The writer is a chartering broker.

11 Which of the following is the LEAST appropriate Korean translation?

① Over the past decade, our revenues have increased by double digit annually.
→ 지난 10년간 당사 수익은 매년 두 자리 수로 증가했습니다.

② Even though the domestic economy has been stagnant this year, we have managed for the third year in a row to sustain a 15% annual growth rate.
→ 올해 국내 경기가 침체되었지만, 당사의 경영은 세번째 해에 드디어 연 15% 성장률을 유지하게 해주었습니다.

③ Your order has been completed and is now ready for shipment. When we receive the credit advice on or before July 21, as agreed, we will ship your order on C/S "Zim Atlantic" leaving Busan on August 6 and reaching Los Angeles on August 17.
→ 주문하신 상품은 완성되어 선적준비가 되어 있습니다. 합의에 따라 7월 21일까지 신용장 통지를 받으면, 8월 6일 부산항을 출항해 8월 17일 Los Angeles에 입항할 예정인 "Zim Atlantic호"에 선적하겠습니다.

④ We have to point out that all the product you are offering must be guaranteed to meet the requirements of the specifications we indicated.
→ 귀사가 제공하는 모든 상품은 당사가 제시한 명세서의 요구에 부합한다는 보증을 해 주셔야 합니다.

12 Which is the LEAST appropriate English-Korean sentence?

① What we're looking for is a year-long contract for the supply of three key components.
→ 오늘 당사가 이루고자 하는 것은 세 가지 주요 부품의 공급에 관한 1년간의 계약을 체결하는 것입니다.

② When do you think we'll get the results of the market analysis? When could we see a return on our investment?
→ 시장 분석결과는 언제쯤 받을 수 있다고 생각합니까? 언제쯤 당사가 돌아와서 다시 투자할 수 있을까요?

③ Most other agencies don't have the expertise to handle our request.
→ 대부분의 다른 대리점은 당사의 요구를 들어줄 만한 전문기술이 없습니다.

④ If the contract is carried out successfully, it will be renewed annually.
→ 계약이 성공적으로 이행되면 1년마다 연장이 될 겁니다.

13 Which of the following is MOST likely to appear right BEFORE the passage below?

> Because we do not sell our garments directly to the consumer, we try to keep our wholesale prices between ourselves and our dealers. It is our way of meriting both the loyalty and good faith of those with whom we do business. Clearly, divulging our wholesale prices to a consumer would be a violation of a trust.
> However, I have enclosed for your reference a list of our dealers in the Bronx and Manhattan. A number of these dealers sell Maxine Sportswear at discount.
> Very truly yours

① If you are interested in importing the products, please feel free to contact us.

② We assure you that our price and quality are the most competitive.

③ We certainly appreciate your interest. Nevertheless, I am afraid I cannot supply you with the information you requested.

④ We regret to inform you that now is not an occasion for price hike.

14 Which of the following insurance documents on the below are acceptable?

> A documentary credit for US$150,000.00 calls for a full set of bills of lading and an insurance certificate to cover all risks. The bill of lading presented indicates an on board date of 15 December.

> A. Policy for US$150,000.00.
> B. Certificate dated 17 December.
> C. Declaration signed by a broker.
> D. Subject to a franchise.

① A + B only
② A + D only
③ B + C only
④ C + D only

15 If the CIF or CIP value cannot be determined from the documents, a nominated bank under UCP 600 will accept an insurance document, which covers :

> A. 110% of the gross amount of the invoice.
> B. 100% of the gross amount of the invoice.
> C. 110% of the documentary credit amount.
> D. 110% of the amount for which payment, acceptance or negotiation is requested under the credit.

① A + C only
② B + D only
③ A + B + D only
④ A + C + D only

16 **What action should the negotiating bank take?**

> A documentary credit advised to a beneficiary payable at sight calls for documents to include an invoice made out in the name of the applicant.
> Documents presented to the negotiating bank by the beneficiary include a customs invoice but not commercial invoice. All other terms and conditions have been met.

① Reject the documents as non-complying.
② Refer to the issuing bank for authority to pay.
③ Return the documents for amendment by the beneficiary.
④ Pay the documents as fully complying with the terms of the credit.

17 **What is NOT appropriate as a reply to customer complaints?**

① Thank you for taking time out of your busy schedule to write us and express your grievances on how our products and services do not meet up with your expectations.
② This is to confirm that I have seen your email. I look forward to receiving my consignment next week as you promised.
③ However, we can neither receive the return nor refund you as you demanded. This is because of our company's policy. We make refunds only for orders whose complaints are received within two weeks of purchase.
④ Despite our effort to deliver your order on time using Skynet Express Delivery Service, it's quite unfortunate that we didn't meet up with the time allotted for the delivery of those products.

18 **What is "This" in the sentences?**

> • This should be located in a conspicuous place to tell the purchases where the product was produced.
> • This is used to clearly indicate to the ultimate purchaser of a product where it is made.

① Packaging
② Country of origin marking
③ Carton number marking
④ Handling caution marking

19 **Which is LEAST proper Korean translation?**

① The selling prices of goods delivered to the customers in exchange are included in the computation of gross sales.
→ 고객에게 교환으로 인도된 상품의 판매가는 매출총액 계산에 포함된다.
② There is an implied warranty by the shipper that the goods are fit for carriage in the ordinary way and are not dangerous.
→ 화물이 통상적인 방법으로 운송에 적합하고 위험하지 않다는 화주의 묵시적 보증이 있다.
③ The consular invoice shall be certified by the consul of the country of destination.
→ 영사송장은 수입국의 영사가 인증하여야 한다.
④ If a bank loan is initially extended with a five-year tenor, after three years, the loan will be said to have a tenor of two years.
→ 만약 은행 대출이 처음에 5년이었는데, 그 후 3년 연장되면, 그 대출은 2년간의 기한이 생겼다고도 말할 수 있다.

20 Which of the following is LEAST correct?

> Dear Ms. Jones :
>
> Thanks for your recent prompt payments. Our records reflect your current account.
>
> Given these circumstances, I am happy to restore your full credit line. In fact, your recent payment record enables me to extend your credit line from the previous US$5,000.00 to US$8,000.00 This will enable you to stock the added inventory you need to accommodate the growing demands of your customers.
>
> On a personal note, I admire your cooperation and appreciate your sincere efforts. You have made my job easier, and I appreciate it.

① The letter offers thanks and praises the customer's good payment record.
② Ms. Jones' company gets a credit extension up to US$13,000.00
③ There is a positive change in the terms of credit.
④ The letter announces that the credit line is now restored.

21 What is the main reason of the letter?

> Dear Corporate Section Manager :
>
> We are writing to inquire about the companies for our products in Bahrain. Your branch in Seoul, Korea, has told us that you may be able to help us. We manufacture radio telephones. At present, we export to Europe and Latin America, but we would like to start exporting to the Arabian Gulf. Could you please forward this letter to any companies in Bahrain that might be interested in representing us? We enclose some of our catalogs.

① to enlarge the branches in Seoul.
② to inquire about an agent in Bahrain
③ to inquire about the radio telephones
④ to export to Europe and Latin America

22 Which is LEAST happening if transaction is conducted as intended below.

> Thank you for the email expressing your interest in our goods, which comes with the Intel xCPU and MS Window CE OS. Our export price is US$250,000.00 CIF LA per unit, and we do have various volume discount plans.

① Seller shall insure the goods with 110% of invoice
② Buyer is responsible for damage of goods in transit
③ Seller may take ICC (C) on the goods which will be delivered
④ Seller shall deliver the goods up to LA at his risk

23 What situation is being explained in the letter below?

> As we wrote you previously about the delays in the delivery of your order, the situation is still the same, the trade union strike is on-going. We apologize for this occurrence, but there is not much that we can do to rectify this, as it is out of our hands.
>
> We again apologize and regret the delay in delivery of your order.

① negotiation with union
② force majeure
③ nonpayment
④ early delivery

[24~25] Read the following and answer.

> A lot of customers have been asking about your bookcase and coffee-table assembly kits. We would like to test the market and have 6 sets of each kit on approval before placing a (ⓐ) order. I can supply trade references if necessary. I attach a (ⓑ) order (No. KM1555) in anticipation of your agreement. There is no hurry but we hope to have your response by the end of April.

24 Why trade references might be needed?

① Because the seller would not trust the buyer in this transaction.

② Because the buyer intends to pay upon arrival of goods.

③ Since the seller requires some references after shipment.

④ Since the buyer would not be satisfied with seller's performance.

25 Which is the best pair for the blanks?

① ⓐ firm – ⓑ provisional

② ⓐ provisional – ⓑ firm

③ ⓐ provisional – ⓑ provisional

④ ⓐ firm – ⓑ firm

<제2과목> 영작문

26 Which of the following BEST fits the blanks?

> A constructive total loss is a situation where the cost of repairs plus the cost of salvage equal or exceed the (ⓐ) of the property, therefore insured property has been abandoned because its actual total loss appears to be unavoidable or because as mentioned above could not be preserved or repaired without an expenditure which would exceed it's value. One example : in the case of damage to the goods, where the cost of repairing the damage and forwarding the goods to their destination would exceed their value on (ⓑ)

① ⓐ cost – ⓑ inspection

② ⓐ value – ⓑ arrival

③ ⓐ cost – ⓑ receipt

④ ⓐ value – ⓑ sales

27 Put best right word(s) in the blank.

> In reference to your letter concerning delayed payment, we wish to inform you that we are accepting your suggestion.
>
> The one condition we would like to add is that if there would be delayed payment beyond what has been agreed upon in the payment schedule and if there is no proper notice given then, we will (   ) to seek legal action against your company.

① have no choice

② be inevitably

③ not help

④ be forced

28 Which CANNOT be included in the underlined these?

> When these are used, the seller fulfills its obligation to deliver when it hands the goods over to the carrier and not when the goods reach the place of destination.

① CPT
② EXW
③ CIF
④ FOB

29 Which of the following is LEAST grammatically appropriate?

> We have received (a) the number of enquiry for floor coverings suitable for use on the rough floors which seem to be a feature of much of the new building (b) taking place in this region.
>
> It would be helpful (c) if you could send us samples showing your range of suitable coverings. A pattern-card of the designs (d) in which they are supplied would also be very useful.

① (a)   ② (b)   ③ (c)   ④ (d)

30 Fill in the blank with the BEST word(s).

> I was very pleased to receive your request of 12 March for waterproof garments on approval. As we have not previously done business together, you will appreciate that I must request either the usual _____, or the name of a bank to which we may refer. As soon as these enquiries are satisfactorily settled we shall be happy to send you a good selection of the items mentioned in your letter.
>
> I sincerely hope that our first transaction will be the beginning of a long and pleasant business association.

① trade references
② credit terms
③ letter of credit
④ bank references

31 Which of the (a) ~ (d) is LEAST appropriate?

> Please correct the following error in my credit report: The loan account number listed for Citizens Bank on the report reads: "137547899." This is incorrect. The correct account number is 137557899.
>
> (a) To verify this information call my branch manager, Len Dane, at 123‑456‑7890.
>
> This correction should change the report (b) by deleting the erroneous statement that says I have twice been late in making payments.
>
> Please (c) open my credit report and (d) send me the corrected clean copy within the next 10 days.

① (a)   ② (b)   ③ (c)   ④ (d)

32 What is best for the blank?

> Thank you for your letter of 15 January regarding our November and December invoice No. 7713
>
> We were sorry to hear about the difficulties you have had, and understand the situation. However, we would appreciate it if you could ( ) the account as soon as possible, as we ourselves have suppliers to pay.
>
> We look forward to hearing from you soon.

① clear

② make

③ debit

④ arrange

33 Which of the following words is NOT appropriate for the blanks below?

> EXW rule places minimum responsibility on the seller, who merely has to make the goods available, suitably packaged, at the specified place, usually the seller's factory or depot.
> The (ⓐ) is responsible for loading the goods onto a vehicle; for all export procedures; for onward transport and for all costs arising after collection of the goods.
> In many cross-border transactions, this rule can present practical difficulties.
> Specifically, the (ⓑ) may still need to be involved in export reporting and clearance processes, and cannot realistically leave these to the (ⓒ). Consider (ⓓ) instead.

① ⓐ exporter

② ⓑ exporter

③ ⓒ buyer

④ ⓓ FCA(seller's premise)

34 Which of the following is the LEAST appropriate one as part of the reply to the letter?

> For a number of years we have imported electric shavers from the United States, but now learn that these shavers can be obtained from British manufacturers. We wish to extend our present range of models and should be glad if you could supply us with a list of British manufacturers likely to be able to help us.
> If you cannot supply the information from your records, could you please refer our enquiry to the appropriate suppliers in London.

① They are the product of the finest materials and workmanship and we offer a worldwide after-sales service.

② We hope you will send us a trial order so that you can test it.

③ We are pleased to inform you that your order was shipped today.

④ We learn that you are interested in electric shavers of British manufacture and enclose our illustrated catalogue and price list.

35 Which of the following is the MOST appropriate English sentence?

> 하지만 당사는 합작투자보다는 기술이전을 선호합니다. 기술이전 계약을 하는 것이 가능한지요? 당사는 기술지향적인 회사입니다.

① We, yet, prefer technology transfer by joint venture. I wonder whether you are in a position to enter into the technology transfer agreement or not. We are a technology-oriented company.

② We, however, prefer technology transfer than joint venture. I wonder if you are in a position to enter the technology transfer agreement. We are a technology-orienting company.

③ We, however, prefer technology transfer to joint venture. I wonder whether you are in a position to enter into the technology transfer agreement. We are a technology-oriented company.

④ We, however, prefer joint venture of technology transfer. I wonder whether you are in a position to enter the technology transfer agreement or not. We are a technology-orienting company.

36 Which of the following has similar meaning for the sentence underlined?

> We are a large music store in Korea and would like to know more about the mobile phones you advertised in this month's edition of "Smart World".
>
> Could you tell us if the mobile phones are out of intellectual property issue and are playable in Korean language? Also please let us know if there are volume discount. We may place a substantial order if the above matters are answered to our satisfaction.

① whether the mobile phones are free from intellectual property issue.

② if the mobile phones are abided by intellectual property problems.

③ provided that the mobile phones are free from intellectual property issue.

④ should the mobile phones are out of intellectual property issue.

[37~38] Read the following letter and answer the questions.

> On behalf of the Board of Directors and Officers of the Stone Corporation, I would like to express sincere appreciation and congratulations to your company for successfully completing the reconstruction of our headquarters building in Incheon, which was devastated by fire last year. Your company has distinguished itself as a leader in the construction industry by performing what appeared to be an almost impossible task. With working under difficult conditions and accelerated construction schedules, your company completed the building as scheduled.

37 Which of the following is the BEST to summarize the underlined sentence above?

① Thanks to your hard work, we could come back to work exactly on the expected date.

② Without your sincere help, the buildings have been restored to its original state perfectly.

③ Although the working plans were tough and tight, your company did fulfill our needs.

④ We had worked hard despite the difficulties, and the construction was finished on time.

38 Which of the following is MOST likely to come after the letter above?

① This accomplishment is attribute to the fine group of professional engineers and skilled craftsmen you assembled on site and to the individual skill and dedication of your project manager, Charles Shin.

② We want to express our deepest appreciation for your hard work during our activities. Your untiring energy and labor made our company the most successful since our foundation began ten years ago.

③ All the people who explored were extremely pleased with your accommodations as well as the friendliness and attentiveness of your entire staff. Please extend my appreciation to the staff and, in particular, to Ms. Han.

④ Please accept my sincere appreciation for the prompt and courteous assistant you gave us in planning the type of event. We were quite pleased with your facility and with the friendly service during the seminar.

[39~40] Read the following letter and answer the questions.

We (ⓐ) to your company by Hills Productions in San Francisco.

Our company produces and distributes (ⓑ) travel and educational DVDs in Korea. These include two 30 minute DVDs on Gyeongju and Buyeo and a 50 minute DVD on Hong Kong. With the overseas market in mind, these (ⓒ) with complete narration and packaging in English.

So far, they have sold very well to tourists in Korea and Hong Kong. We would now like to market the DVDs directly in the United States. We feel that potential markets for these DVDs are travel agencies, video stores, book stores, schools and libraries.

We would appreciate your advice on whether your company would be interested in acting as a (ⓓ) in the United States or if you have any recommendations on any other American associates.

(ⓔ) for your evaluation. We look forward to your reply.

39 Which of the following does NOT fit in the blanks?

① ⓐ were referred
② ⓑ a number of
③ ⓒ have also produced
④ ⓓ distributor

40 Which is MOST suitable for the underlined (ⓔ)?

① Enclosed are English copies of the DVDs
② Same samples are produced
③ Like other agencies, we send originals
④ Originals and copies of sample are attached

41 Choose a different intention from others.

① We shall have to cancel the order, and take all necessary actions for the claim for delayed shipment.
② As you have shipped a machine damaged packaging, all costs of the repairs should be borne by your company.
③ You're requested to substitute any damaged products by brand-new products packed properly at your expense. Otherwise, we have no choice but to raise a claim for a bad packing.
④ It's our regret to inform you that some boxes are terribly broken due to a bad packing. We found that several products seemed to be replaced promptly as they were damaged, bended, and even broken.

42 Below is a part of meeting memo between a seller and a buyer. Which CANNOT be inferred?

Point Discussed and Agreed
1) Both parties have agreed to sell and purchase 100 units of the control box for US $500,000.00
2) Robert Corporation should make an irrevocable Letter of Credit issued payable at sight in favor of Hannam International by OCT 27, 2018.
3) Hannam International should ship the above products within two months after receiving the L/C from Robert Corporation.

① Robert Corporation agreed to buy some control boxes.
② Hannam International would be a beneficiary of the L/C.
③ Robert Corporation would be a drawee of the Bill of Exchange.
④ Robert Corporation would be an applicant of the L/C.

43 Which is most AWKWARD English writing?

① 당사가 주문을 했을 때, 귀사는 3월 2일까지 FB–900의 선적을 마칠 수 있다고 보장했습니다.

→ When we placed the order, you guaranteed us that you could finish the shipment of FB–900 no later than March 2.

② 오늘 주문서 no.4587의 배송을 받고 상자를 개봉하자, 당사는 보내주신 상품의 일부가 없어졌음을 발견했습니다.

→ Today we received delivery of order no.4587, and on opening the box, we discovered some of the items were missing.

③ 향후 4주간 그 품목의 재고 확보를 기대할 수 없으므로, 이를 대신할 상품들을 제공해 드리고자 합니다.

→ We do not anticipate having inventory of the item for another 4 weeks, so we would like to suggest some alternatives for it.

④ 당사는 귀사의 주문서에 언급된 냉장고(Model no.876)의 재고가 없음을 알려드리게 되어 유감으로 생각합니다.

→ We regret to inform you that the refrigerators(Model no.876) mentioning in your order is not in stock.

[44-45] Read the following and answer.

> May we draw your attention to special discount which are given to our most valued customers for bulk purchases.
>
> These discounts comprise 5% for order over US $10,000.00 10% for orders over US$50,000.00 and 15% for orders over US$100,000.00 As your company has always placed sizeable orders with us, we hope you take advantage of this event.
>
> We look forward to continued business relationship with you.

44 What amount of discount is allowed when US $10,000.00 worth order is placed?

① $9,500.00

② $5,000.00

③ $500.00

④ nothing

45 What can be best replacement for the underlined sizeable?

① minimum ② average

③ small ④ large

46 What is best written for the blank?

> There is still some risk in D/P transaction where a sight draft is used to control transferring the title of a shipment. The buyer's ability or willingness to pay might change from the time the goods are shipped until the time the drafts are presented for payment;
>
> (   )

① the presenter is liable for the buyer's payment.

② the seller shall ask the presenting bank to ship back the goods.

③ the carrier ask the buyer to provide indemnity for release of the goods.

④ there is no bank promise to pay.

47 What does the following explain?

A provision in the contract of insurance which specifies a minimum of damage which must occur to the property insured for the insurer to be liable;
where such specified cover is reached, the insurer then becomes liable for all the damages suffered as a consequence of a peril insured against.

① deduction   ② limit

③ immunity   ④ franchise

48 What is NOT true about Incoterms 2010?

① Under EXW rule, the seller has no obligation to the buyer to load the goods.

② Under FCA rule, the seller is not responsible to the buyer for loading the goods at the seller's premises.

③ Under CIF rule, the seller is responsible for delivery of the goods at the agreed place of shipment.

④ Under DAT rule, the seller is obliged to unload the goods at the terminal at the named port or place of destination.

49 Which has the LEAST proper explanation?

① Negotiable B/L – Bills of lading which are made out to one's order.

② Received B/L – A bill of lading evidencing that the goods have been received into the care of the carrier, but not yet loaded on board.

③ Foul B/L – A bill of lading which has been not qualified by the carrier to show that the goods were not sound when unloaded.

④ Straight B/L – A bill of lading which stipulates that the goods are to be delivered only to the named consignee.

50 Which pair does NOT have similar meaning?

① Your bank has been given to us as a reference by Brown&Co.
→ Brown&Co. have been referred by our bank to you.

② Please inform us of their credit standing.
→ Please furnish us with information about their credit status.

③ We will treat your information in strict confidence.
→ Your information will be treated as absolutely confidential.

④ We have had no previous dealings with the above company.
→ We have not had any business transactions with the above company so far.

<제3과목> 무역실무

51 신용장거래 중 은행의 서류심사기준에 관한 설명으로 옳지 않은 것은?

① 지정은행, 확인은행, 개설은행은 서류가 문면상 일치하는지 여부를 서류만으로 심사해야 한다.

② 운송서류는 신용장의 유효기일 이내, 그리고 선적일 후 21일 이내에 제시되어야 한다.

③ 신용장에서 요구되지 아니한 서류는 무시되며, 제시자에게 반환될 수 있다.

④ 서류상의 화주 또는 송화인은 반드시 신용장의 수익자이어야 한다.

52 매도인의 계약위반과 이에 대한 구제의 방법이 아닌 것은?

① 물품이 계약에 부적합한 경우 계약에 적합한 물품의 가액에 대한 비율에 따라 대금을 감액할 수 있다.

② 매수인은 매도인의 의무이행을 위하여 상당한 기간만큼의 추가기간을 지정할 수 있다.

③ 매도인이 상당한 기간 내에 그 물품명세를 지정하지 아니할 때는 매수인이 스스로 이를 확정할 수 있다.

④ 매도인이 약정된 기일 전에 물품을 인도한 경우, 매수인은 인도를 수령하거나 거절할 수 있다.

53 고지의무위반과 담보위반에 대한 다음 설명 중 적절하지 않은 것은?

① 고지내용은 실질적으로 충족되면 고지의무 위반으로 보지 않는다.

② 피보험자가 고지의무의 중요한 사항을 위반하면 보험계약이 취소될 수 있지만, 담보위반은 보험계약이 해지될 수 있다.

③ 고지의무 위반은 보험계약이 무효가 될 수 있고, 담보위반은 위반시점 이후의 계약이 무효가 될 수 있다.

④ 고지의무 위반의 경우는 보험료가 일부 반환되나, 담보위반은 보험료가 전부 반환된다.

54 다음 서류 제목 중, 신용장이 요구하는 송장(Invoice)으로 인정할 수 없는 것은 무엇인가?

① Consular Invoice

② Tax Invoice

③ Provisional Invoice

④ Customs Invoice

55 다음 중 연관성이 있는 것끼리만 연결된 것을 고르시오.

> ㉠ Container B/L
> ㉡ Consolidation
> ㉢ Container Freight Station
> ㉣ Less than Container Loaded Cargo
> ㉤ House B/L

① ㉠, ㉡, ㉢, ㉣

② ㉠, ㉡, ㉢, ㉤

③ ㉠, ㉡, ㉣, ㉤

④ ㉡, ㉢, ㉣, ㉤

56 권리포기 선화증권(Surrendered B/L)에 관한 내용으로 옳은 것은?

① 원본의 선화증권을 의미한다.

② non-negotiable이다.

③ 주로 중계무역 시에 사용한다.

④ 권리증권이다.

57 B/L상에 기재된 화물은 다음과 같다. 이와 관련된 설명으로 가장 관련이 적은 것을 고르시오.

> GROUND GRANULATED BLAST FURNACE
> SLAG 30,000 M/T
> PACKING TO BE IN JUMBO BAGS OF 1.5 M. TON
> WITH TOLERANCE OF +/− 10 PERCENT IN
> EACH BAGS

① CHARTER PARTY B/L이다.

② 하역비용은 선사가 부담하게 된다.

③ 화물이 담긴 점보백의 총 개수는 2만개이다.

④ 각 점보백의 중량은 1.35톤~1.65톤 범위 이내이어야 한다.

58 결제방식에 대한 다음 설명 중 옳지 않은 것은?

① 수출입은행은 선적 후 무역금융으로서 수출팩토링, 포페이팅, 수출환어음매입 제도를 운영하고 있다.

② 수출팩토링은 수출채권을 수출기업으로부터 상환청구권 없이 매입하는 수출금융상품이다.

③ 포페이팅은 수출의 대가로 받은 어음을 수출업자에게 상환청구권 없이 고정금리로 할인하는 금융기법이다.

④ 포페이터는 환어음에 추가하는 지급확약(Aval)을 담보로 활용하며 수출상에게도 별도의 보증을 요구한다.

59 화환신용장방식에 의한 매입 관련 주의사항으로 옳지 않은 것은?

① 유효기일이 은행의 영업일이 아닐 경우, 그 다음 영업일까지 유효기일이 연장된다.

② 매입은 서류제시기간 이내로서 유효기일 이내에 이루어져야 한다.

③ 매입을 위하여 은행이 지정된 경우 지정은행이 아닌 수익자의 거래은행에 유효기일까지 서류를 제시하면 하자이다.

④ General L/C의 경우 지정된 은행에서 매입절차를 진행해야 하지만, 지정은행이 아닌 수출상의 거래은행에 매입을 의뢰할 경우 재매입절차가 필요하다.

60 복합운송의 기본요건에 대한 설명으로 옳지 않은 것은?

① 운송책임의 단일성

② 복합운송증권의 발행

③ 단일운임의 설정

④ 복합운송인의 이종의 운송수단 보유

61 해상보험계약의 법률적 성격으로 옳지 않은 것은?

① 낙성계약

② 요식계약

③ 부합계약

④ 쌍무계약

62 해상보험에 대한 설명으로 옳지 않은 것은?

① 일부보험은 보험금액이 보험가액보다 많은 경우를 말한다.

② 전부보험은 보험금액과 보험가액이 같은 경우를 말한다.

③ 초과보험은 실제로 초과보험이 인정된다면 도덕적 위태가 발생할 수 있으므로 고의에 의한 초과보험은 무효로 우리나라 상법에서 규정하고 있다.

④ 병존보험은 동일한 피보험목적물에 수개의 보험계약이 존재하는 경우이다.

63 양도가능신용장에 관한 설명으로 옳은 것은?

① 신용장 양도와 관련하여 발생한 모든 수수료는 제2수익자가 지급해야 한다.

② 개설은행은 양도은행이 될 수 없다.

③ 제2수익자에 의한 또는 그를 위한 제시는 양도은행에 대하여 이루어져야 한다.

④ 양도된 신용장은 제2수익자의 요청에 의하여 수회양도될 수 있다.

64 신용장 문구가 "available with ANY BANK by negotiation of your draft at 180 days after sight for 100 percent of invoice value."일 때 발행은행인 KOOKMIN BANK가 해외의 매입은행에게 대금을 즉시 지급하고, 수출업자가 선적 후 즉시 대금 지급을 받는 경우를 무엇이라 하는가?

① Shipper's usance

② Domestic banker's usance

③ Overseas banker's usance

④ European D/P

65 내국신용장이나 구매확인서에 대한 설명으로 옳지 않은 것은?

① 수출신용장은 Master L/C, 내국신용장은 Local L/C라고 한다.

② 원신용장이 양도신용장인 경우에 한하여 내국신용장 발급이 가능하다.

③ 내국신용장으로 국내에서 물품을 공급받는 경우 부가가치세 영세율이 적용된다.

④ 구매확인서와 달리 내국신용장은 개설은행의 지급확약이 있다.

66 은행이 서류심사를 할 때 신용장 상의 표현과 엄격일치가 적용되는 서류는?

① 상업송장

② 원산지증명서

③ 선화증권

④ 포장명세서

67 대외무역법상의 특정거래형태에 관한 설명으로 옳지 않은 것은?

① 위탁판매거래는 수출자가 물품의 소유권을 수입자에게 이전하지 않고 수출한 후 판매된 범위 내에서만 대금을 영수한다.

② 외국인수수입은 물품을 외국에서 조달하여 외국의 사업현장에서 인수하고 그 대금을 국내에서 지급하는 거래방식이다.

③ 중계무역의 경우 수수료를 대가로 물품과 선적서류가 최초 수출자에게서 최종수입자에게 직접 인도된다.

④ 위탁가공무역은 가공임을 지급하는 조건으로 가공 후 국내에 재수입하거나 제3국에 판매하는 수출입거래이다.

68 아래 글상자는 항공운임 관련 부대운임 중 무엇에 대한 설명인가?

> 항공화물운임을 후불로 항공운송대리점에 지불할 경우 항공운송대리점이 환전 및 송금에 필요한 경비를 보전하기 위해 징구하는 요금을 말하며, 보통 인보이스 금액의 2%를 징구하며 최소 10달러를 징구한다.

① Handling Charge

② Documentation Fee

③ Collect Charge Fee

④ Terminal Handling Charge

69 신용장상에 "available with issuing bank by payment"라는 문구가 의미하는 것은?

① 거래은행을 통하여 발행은행에게 지급을 요청한다.

② 일람불 환어음을 발행하여 상환은행에 매입을 요청한다.

③ 기한부 환어음을 발행하여 발행은행에 지급을 요청한다.

④ 일람불 환어음을 발행하여 발행은행에 인수를 요청한다.

70 국제팩터링(International Factoring)의 수입국 팩터(Import factor)에 대한 설명으로 옳지 않은 것은?

① 수입국에서 수입자와 국제팩터링계약을 체결하다.

② 수입자의 외상수입을 위하여 신용승낙의 위험을 인수한다.

③ 팩터링채권을 회수하고 전도금융을 제공한다.

④ 수출팩터에게 송금하는 팩터링회사를 말한다.

71 외국중재판정의 승인과 집행을 위한 뉴욕협약(1958)상의 요건으로 옳게 설명하고 있는 것은?

① 중재판정의 승인과 집행국 이외에 영토에서 내려진 중재판정은 제외한다.

② 중재판정이 이루어진 후에는 중재합의가 무효라 해도 승인 및 집행이 가능하다.

③ 중재판정이 공서양속에 반하는 때에는 중재판정의 승인과 집행이 거부될 수 있다.

④ 중재판정이 구속력을 가지지 않아야 한다.

72 무역클레임의 간접적 발생원인이 아닌 것은?

① 상관습 및 법률의 상이

② 계약의 유효성 문제

③ 이메일 사용 시 전달과정상의 오류

④ 언어의 상위

73 신용장 통일규칙(UCP 600)상 보험서류의 발행요건에 관한 설명 중 옳지 않은 것은?

① 보험서류는 문면상 필요하거나 요구가 있는 경우에는, 원본은 모두 정당하게 서명되어 있어야 한다.

② 보험서류는 필요한 경우 보험금을 지급하도록 지시하는 당사자의 배서가 나타나 있어야 한다.

③ 보험서류의 피보험자가 지정되지 않은 경우, 화주나 수익자 지시식으로 발행하되 배서가 있어야 한다.

④ 신용장에서 보험증권이 요구된 경우, 보험증명서나 포괄예정보험 확정통지서를 제시하여도 충분하다.

74 신용장거래에서 서류상의 일자(date)에 관한 설명으로서 옳지 않은 것은?

① 신용장상에 일자의 요구가 없더라도 환어음, 운송서류, 보험서류 등은 반드시 일자가 있어야 한다.

② 선적전검사증명서(PSI)는 반드시 선적일자 이전의 일자에 발행된 사실이 나타나 있어야 한다.

③ "Within 2 days of"는 어떠한 사실 이전의 2일에서 동 사실 이후의 2일까지의 기간을 말한다.

④ 서류는 준비일자와 함께 서명일자가 따로 명시되어 있는 경우, 서명일자에 발행된 것으로 본다.

75 신용장에서 무고장의 운송서류(clean transport document)가 요구된 경우, 운송서류상의 다음과 같은 문언 중에서 인수가능한 것은?

① Packaging is not sufficient.

② Packaging contaminated

③ Goods damaged/scratched.

④ Packaging may be insufficient.

<제1과목> 영문해석

※ **Below are correspondences between buyer and seller.**

> This is to inform you that we received the shipment of Celltopia on December 15. Our technicians have thoroughly tested all the machines and found 25 defective batteries. We listed the serial numbers of them in the attached sheet.

> We have already sent the replacement batteries via Fedex.
> Meanwhile, please send us the defective ones at our cost. You may use our Fedex account.

01 Which can NOT be inferred from the above?

① Defective batteries have their own serial numbers.
② Replacement batteries have been sent via courier service.
③ Buyer will pay freight for the returning batteries.
④ Seller agrees that some of their products were against the sales contract.

02 Which can be inferred from the below?

> Several of my customers have recently expressed an interest in your remote controlled window blinds, and have enquired about its quality.
>
> We are a wide distributor of window blinds in Asia. If quality and price are satisfactory, there are prospects of good sales here.
>
> However, before placing an order I should be glad if you would send me a selection of your remote-controlled window blinds on 20 days' approval. Any of the items unsold at the end of this period and which I decide not to keep as stock would be returned at our expense.
>
> I hope to hear from you soon.
>
> Alex Lee
> HNC International

① Alex shall pay for the goods 20 days after arrival of goods.
② Alex has confidence on the window blinds, so cash with order is acceptable.
③ Freight for the returning goods will be borne by HNC International.
④ Seller shall deliver the goods within 20 days after order.

03 Which does NOT belong to 'some documents' underlined below?

> Some documents commonly used in relation to the transportation of goods are not considered as transport documents under UCP 600.

① Delivery Order
② Forwarder's Certificate of Receipt
③ Forwarder's Certificate of Transport
④ Forwarder's Bill of Lading

04 In accordance with UCP 600, which of the following alterations can a first beneficiary request to a transferring bank to make under a transferable L/C?

① Extend the expiry date

② Decrease the unit price

③ Extend the period for shipment

④ Decrease insurance cover

[05 ~ 06] Read the following and answer.

Dear Mr. Han,

Thank you for your enquiry about our French Empire range of drinking glasses. There is a revival of interest in this period, so we are not surprised that these products have become popular with your customers.

I am sending this fax pp. 1-4 of our catalogue with CIF Riyadh prices, as you said you would like an immediate preview of this range. I would appreciate your comments on the designs with regard to your market.

I look forward to hearing from you.

05 What kind of transaction is implied?

① a reply to a trade enquiry

② a firm offer

③ an acceptance of an offer

④ a rejection of an offer

06 Which is NOT similar to the underlined with regard to?

① regarding

② about

③ concerning

④ in regard for

07 What would Jenny's representative do on the coming visit?

Dear Jenny,

With reference to our phone conversation this morning, I would like one of your representatives to visit our store at 443 Teheran Road, Seoul to give an estimate for a complete refit. Please could you contact me to arrange an appointment?

As mentioned on the phone, it is essential that work should be completed before the end of February 2018, and this would be stated in the contract.

I attach the plans and specifications.

① offer

② credit enquiry

③ trade enquiry

④ compensation

[08 ~ 09] Read the following and answer.

A sight draft is used when the exporter wishes to retain title to the shipment until it reaches its destination and payment is made.
In actual practice, the ocean bill of lading is endorsed by the exporter and sent via the exporter's bank to the buyer's bank. It is accompanied by the sight draft with invoices, and other shipping documents that are specified by either the buyer or the buyer's country (e.g., packing lists, consular invoices, insurance certificates). The foreign bank notifies the buyer when it has received these documents. As soon as the draft is paid, the (A) foreign bank turns over the bill of lading thereby enabling the buyer to obtain the shipment.

08 Which payment method is inferred from the above?

① Sight L/C

② D/P

③ Usance L/C

④ D/A

09 What is the appropriate name for the (A) <u>foreign bank</u>?

① collecting bank   ② remitting bank

③ issuing bank   ④ nego bank

10 Which of the following BEST completes the blanks in the letter?

> We would like to send (A) - Heathrow (B) Seoul, Korea, 12 crates of assorted glassware, to be delivered (C) the next 10 days.

① ex – to – within

② ex – to – off

③ from – through – within

④ from – through – above

11 What is the appropriate title of the document for the following?

> Whereas you have issued a Bill of Lading covering the above shipment and the above cargo has been arrived at the above port of discharge (or the above place of delivery), we hereby request you to give delivery of the said cargo to the above mentioned party without production of the original Bill of Lading.

① Fixture Note

② Trust Receipt

③ Letter of Guarantee

④ Letter of Indemnity

12 What is TRUE about the CPT term of the Incoterms 2010?

① The seller delivers the goods to the carrier or another person nominated by the buyer at an agreed place.

② The seller fulfils its obligation to deliver when the goods reach the place of destination.

③ If several carriers are used for the carriage and the parties do not agree on a specific point of delivery, risk passes when the goods have been delivered to the first carrier at a point entirely of the seller's choosing.

④ If the seller incurs costs under its contract of carriage related to unloading at the named place of destination, the seller is entitled to recover such costs from the buyer.

13 Which is LEAST proper Korean translation?

① The Manufacturer grants to the HNC the exclusive and nontransferable franchise.

→ 제조사는 HNC에게 독점적 양도불능 체인영업권을 부여한다.

② Despite its diminished luster, Apple remains the most valuable U.S. company with a market value of USD432 billion.

→ 비록 빛을 다소 잃기는 했어도 애플사는 432억불의 시장가치를 가진 가장 값진 미국 회사로 남아 있다.

③ Rejection of nonconforming goods should be made by a buyer in a reasonable time after the goods are delivered.

→ 불일치 상품의 인수거절은 상품이 인도된 후 합리적인 기간 내에 매수인이 해야 한다.

④ Please sign and return the duplicate to seller after confirming this sales contract.

→ 이 매매 계약서를 확인한 후 서명하고 그 부본을 매도자에게 보내 주십시오.

14 What is the writer's purpose?

> ....Your prices are not competitive and therefore we are unable to place an order with you at this time, even though we are favorably impressed with your samples⋯⋯. Under such circumstances, we have to ask for your most competitive prices on the particular item, your sample No.10 which is in high demand.
> We trust you will make every effort to revise your prices.

① an acceptance of an offer

② a trade inquiry

③ an inquiry to search a new product

④ a purchase order

15 The following is about CIF, Incoterms 2010. Choose the wrong one.

① The seller delivers the goods on board the vessel or procures the goods already so delivered.

② The seller must contract for and pay the costs and freight necessary to bring the goods to the named port of destination.

③ The seller contracts for insurance cover for the seller's risk of loss of or damage to the goods during the carriage.

④ The buyer should note that the seller is required to obtain insurance only on minimum cover.

16 What is LEAST correct about a distributor and an agent?

① A distributor is an independently owned business that is primarily involved in wholesaling.

② A distributor doesn't take title to the goods that he's distributing.

③ The agent's role is to get orders and usually earn a commission for his services.

④ The initial investment and costs of doing business as an agent are lower than those of doing business as a distributor.

17 What does the following explain?

> The purchase of a series of credit instruments such as drafts drawn under usance letters of credit, bills of exchange, promissory notes, or other freely negotiable instruments on a "nonrecourse" basis.

① forfeiting

② factoring

③ negotiation

④ confirmation

18 What is NOT correct about the FAS rule of the Incoterms 2010?

① Where merchandise is sold on an FAS basis, the cost of the goods includes delivery to alongside the vessel.

② Seller is responsible for any loss or damage, or both, until the goods have been delivered alongside the vessel.

③ Buyer must give seller adequate notice of name, sailing date, loading berth of, delivery time to, the vessel.

④ Buyer is not responsible for any loss or damage, while the goods are on a lighter conveyance alongside the vessel within reach of its loading tackle.

19 What is NOT correct about the CIF rule of the Incoterms 2010?

① Where merchandise is sold on a CIF basis, the price includes the cost of the goods, insurance coverage and freight to the named port of destination.

② Seller must provide and pay for transportation to named port of destination.

③ Seller must pay export taxes, or other fees or charges, if any, levied because of exportation.

④ Buyer must receive the goods upon shipment, handle and pay for all subsequent movement of the goods.

20 Under the UCP 600, what is the obligation of the issuing bank?

> A documentary credit pre-advice was issued on 1 March for USD 510,000 with the following terms and conditions:
>
> - Partial shipment allowed
> - Latest shipment date 30 April
> - Expiry date 15 May
>
> On 2 March the applicant requested amendments prohibiting partial shipment and extending the expiry date to 30 May.

① Clarify with the beneficiary the period for presentation.
② Issue the documentary credit as originally instructed.
③ Issue the documentary credit incorporating all the amendments.
④ Issue the documentary credit incorporating the extended expiry date only.

21 Which of the following is LEAST inferred?

> Dear Mr. Smith
> We appreciate receiving your order for 1,000 XTM-500 linear circuit amplifiers.
> Our credit department has approved a credit line of USD 10,000 for you. Because the total on your current order exceeds this limit, we need at least partial payment (half up front) to ship the goods to your factory.
> If you anticipate more purchases of this size, call me and we'll see what we can do about extending your limit. We value your business, hope this is a satisfactory solution, and thank you for the opportunity to serve you.
> Sincerely yours,
> John Denver

① John requires minimum USD 4,500 cash for accepting this order.
② Mr. Smith must have ordered the products for more than USD 10,000.
③ The seller is granting credit, but not in the amount the customer wants.
④ John explains the balance required to deliver the entire order, and invite the customer to further discuss extending the credit limit.

22 Which of the following is NOT acceptable as the maturity date for the draft below?

> A documentary credit is issued for an amount of USD 60,000 and calls for drafts to be drawn at 30 days from bill of lading date. Documents have been presented with a bill of lading dated 09 November 2018. (09 November + 30 days = 09 December)

① 09 December 2018
② 30 days from bill of lading date
③ 30 days after 09 November 2018
④ December 9th, 2018

23 Which explains "pro-forma invoice" correctly?

① It is a commercial bill demanding payment for the goods sold.

② It is usually issued by diplomatic officials of the importing country to verify the export price.

③ It is completed on a special form of the importing country to enable the goods to pass through the customs of that country.

④ It is a preliminary bill of sale sent to buyer in advance of a shipment or delivery of goods.

24 Which is CORRECT about the letter?

> Enclosed please find a CI nonmetallic wind shifter, model BRON-6SJ7. As we discussed on the telephone, the device has recently developed a noticeable skew to the west.
>
> You suggested that we send the unit to your attention for evaluation and an estimate of the cost of repair of the unit. Please call me when you have that estimate; we will decide at that time whether it makes sense to repair the device or to purchase a new model.

① The letter is from Production Department to shipping company.

② The letter is from shipping company to Production Department.

③ The letter is from Customer Service to customer.

④ The letter is from customer to Customer Service.

25 What is NOT a good example in consideration of the following?

> In international trade, the seller should make certain that the essential elements of the contract are clearly stated in the communications exchanged by the buyer.

① The description of goods shall include the HS Code of exporting country.

② The purchase price and the terms of payment should be stated.

③ The terms of delivery should be set out.

④ Instructions for transportation and insurance is to be specified.

<제2과목> 영작문

26 Which is most AWKWARD English writing?

① 이번 지불 연기를 허락해 주신다면 정말 감사하겠습니다.
→ We would be very grateful if you could allow us the postponement of this payment.

② 귀사가 품질 보증서를 보내주실 수 없다면, 주문을 취소할 수밖에 없습니다.
→ If you cannot send us a guaranty, we will have no choice but canceling the order.

③ 매도인은 매수인의 요구조건에 따라 매도인 스스로 물품명세를 작성한다.
→ The Seller makes the specification himself in accordance with the requirements of the Buyer.

④ 매수인은 판촉에 대한 책임을 진다.
→ Buyer shall be responsible for sales promotion.

[27 ~ 28] Read the following and answer.

We are a chain of retailers based in Birmingham and are looking for a manufacturer who can supply us with a wide range of sweaters for the men's leisurewear market. We were impressed by the new designs displayed on your stand at the Hamburg Menswear Exhibition last month.

As we usually (ⓐ) large orders, we would expect a quantity discount in addition to a 20% trade discount off net list prices. Our terms of payment are normally 30-day bill of exchange, D/A.

If these conditions interest you, and you can (ⓑ) orders of over 500 garments at one time, please send us your current catalogue and price list.

We hope to hear from you soon.

27 Which is best rewritten for the underlined sentence?

① If you can meet these conditions,
② Provided that if we can meet these conditions,
③ Should you need interest to these conditions in advance,
④ If the interest brings you to the conditions above,

28 Which is the best pair for the blanks?

① ⓐ take − ⓑ meet
② ⓐ place − ⓑ meet
③ ⓐ take − ⓑ provide
④ ⓐ place − ⓑ provide

[29 ~ 30] Read the following and answer.

We would like to place an order on behalf of Tokyo Jewelers Inc.
Please ( ) 5,000 uncut diamonds and once it is available, Tokyo Jewelers will surely buy it to be forwarded at the Quanstock Diamond Mine. We really would appreciate if you could accommodate this order.

Hans International

29 Fill in the blank with a suitable word.

① repair   ② replace
③ reserve   ④ revoke

30 Who is mostly likely to be Hans International?

① buying agent   ② selling agent
③ importer   ④ exporter

[31 ~ 32] Read the following and answer.

In reference to your order No. 458973, we regret to inform you that we cannot supply the goods that were stated therein due to an outstanding ( ) from your preceding order. So far we have received no reply from you concerning this outstanding amount.

We are very disappointed about this fact, and hope that you can help us to clear out this problem, very soon. Should you have any comments regarding payments, we should appreciate hearing from you.

Please give this matter an immediate attention. We, therefore, expect to receive remittance without any further delay, before we can process future orders.

31 What is the most appropriate word for the blank?

① balance   ② order
③ offer   ④ complaint

32 Rephrase the underlined sentence.

① settle the discrepancy

② settle the overdue amount

③ pay the money in advance

④ pay interest first

33 How many televisions were expected to be unloaded at the port of destination?

> Thank you for the fast dispatch of our order, but I regret to inform you that, unfortunately you have not completed our order, three of the televisions were missing, and only 34 were received.
>
> We will be happy to receive a credit note for the missing goods or three televisions in this discrepancy.

① 3   ② 31   ③ 34   ④ 37

34 Which of the following BEST fits the blank?

> (   ) comprehends all loss occasioned to ship, freight, and cargo, which has not been wholly or partly sacrificed for the common safety or which does not otherwise come under the heading of general average or total loss.

① Abandonment

② Average

③ Particular average

④ Marine adventure

[35 ~ 36] Read the following and answer.

> I would like your quotation for silicon used in automobile keypads with the following park number :
>
> K0A11164B – 100,000pcs.
> K0A50473A – 200,000pcs.
>
> We require keypads appropriate for Mercedes Benz and Ford. It would be (   ) if you could state your prices, including delivery up to our works. Delivery would be required within three weeks from order date.
>
> Peter Han
> K- Hans International

35 What is suitable for the blank?

① appreciated

② delayed

③ depreciated

④ appreciating

36 Which rules of the Incoterms 2010 would be applied for the above situation?

① D terms

② E term

③ C terms

④ F terms

37 What is (A)?

> The more geographic reach your company has, the more important (A) this clause will become. For example, if you're a small local business dealing 100% exclusively with locals, you may not really need a clause telling your customers which law applies.
>
> Now, take a big corporation with customers and offices in numerous countries around the world. If a customer in Japan wants to sue over an issue with the product, would Japanese law apply or would the law from any of the other countries take over? Or, what if you're a Korea-based business that has customers from Europe.
>
> In both cases, (A) this clause will declare which laws will apply and can keep both companies from having to hire international lawyers.

① Arbitration Clause
② Governing Law Clause
③ Severability Clause
④ Infringement Clause

38 Fill in the blanks with the MOST proper word(s) in common.

> (ⓐ) cannot be final if a contract is subsequently made on suppliers' term such as ; all (ⓑ) are subject to confirmations and acceptance by us upon receipt of an order and will not be binding unless so confirmed by us in writing.

① ⓐ Quotations, ⓑ quotations
② ⓐ Letters of credit, ⓑ letters of credit
③ ⓐ Invoices, ⓑ invoices
④ ⓐ Contracts, ⓑ contracts

[39~40] Read the following and answer the questions.

> We were pleased to receive your fax order of 29 June and have arranged to ship the electric shavers by SS Tyrania leaving London on 6 July and due to arrive at Sidon on the 24th.
>
> As the urgency of your order left no time to make the usual enquiries, we are compelled to place this transaction this way and have drawn on you through Midminster Bank Ltd for the amount of the enclosed invoice. The bank will instruct their correspondent in Sidon to pass ⓐ _____ to you against payment of the draft.
>
> Special care has been taken to select items suited to your local conditions. We hope you will find them satisfactory and that your present order will be the first of many.

39 What is the underlined 'this way'?

① D/P
② on credit
③ by letter of credit
④ by cash

40 What is the most appropriate word(s) for the blank ⓐ?

① the bill of lading
② invoice
③ credit reference
④ letter of credit

41 Which is best rewritten for the underlined words?

> We received your email of October 20 requesting a reduction in price for our Celltopia II. Your request has been carefully considered, but we regret that it is not possible to allow a discount at this time due to the recent appreciation of Korean won against US dollar.

① we are not acceptable to discount at this moment
② we are not in a position to discount at this moment
③ it is discounted for this time
④ it is discountable this time

42 What is the most appropriate for the blank?

> We regret to inform you that payment of USD 75,000 has not been made for order No. 3038.
>
> We sent your company a (   ) notice three weeks ago, and so far we have received no reply from you. We hope that you can help us to clear this amount immediately.

① shipping

② payment

③ check

④ reminder

43 Which is NOT similar to the underlined (A)?

> This is (A) in reference to product No. 34. Our supplier has informed us that there is a price increase due to the increase in the price of materials used for this product.

① With reference to

② With regard to

③ As per

④ Regarding

[44~45] Read the following and answer.

> We have gained an impressive exports contract of USD 100 million TV monitors. For this, we will need a fund for machinery and materials that will be used on this contract. Due to this massive outlay, we are requesting for an increase in our company's credit limit from USD 30 million to USD 50 million.
>
> ~~~~~~~~~~~~~~~~~~~
>
> With reference to your letter, we are pleased to advise that the credit limit is (A   ) as per your request with effect from 1 November 2019. However please note that (B) the interest rate will be increased from 6.5% to 7.5%.

44 Which is best for the blank (A)?

① increased by USD 20 million

② improved to USD 20 million

③ decreased by USD 20 million

④ between USD 30 million to USD 50 million

45 Rephrase the underlined (B)

① we will raise the interest rate from 6.5% to 7.5%

② we will rise the interest rate from 6.5% to 7.5%

③ the interest rate will exceed 6.5% for 1.0%

④ the interest rate will surpass 7.5% from 1.0%

[46~47] Read the following and answer.

Dear Mr. Hong,

Thank you for your letter of 15 October concerning the damage to the goods against Invoice No.1555. I can confirm that the goods were checked before they left our warehouse, so it appears that the damage occurred during shipment.

Please could you return the goods to us, carriage forward?
We will send a refund as soon as we receive them.

Please accept my (   ) for the inconvenience caused.

Yours sincerely

46 **What can NOT be inferred from the letter above?**

① Seller wants to pay freight for retuning goods.
② Buyer claimed for the goods damaged.
③ Goods were in good order at seller's warehouse.
④ Seller would like to replace goods.

47 **Put the right word in the blank.**

① thanks   ② regards
③ apologies   ④ relief

48 **Fill in the blank with suitable word.**

Sellers must trust that the bank issuing the letter of credit is sound, and that the bank will pay as agreed. If sellers have any doubts, they can use a (   ) letter of credit, which means that another (presumably more trustworthy) bank will undertake payment.

① confirmed   ② irrevocable
③ red-clause   ④ None of the above

49 **Fill in the blank with suitable word.**

A _____ letter of credit allows the beneficiary to receive partial payment before shipping the products or performing the services. Originally these terms were written in red ink, hence the name. In practical use, issuing banks will rarely offer these terms unless the beneficiary is very creditworthy or any advising bank agrees to refund the money if the shipment is not made.

① simple   ② anticipatory
③ black   ④ None of the above

50 **What is best for the blank?**

We are a large engineering company exporting machine parts worldwide, and have a contract to supply a Middle Eastern customer for the next two years.

As the parts we will be supplying are similar in nature and are going to the same destination over this period for USD 50,000,000 annually.

Would you be willing to provide (   ) against all risks for this period?

We look forward to hearing from you.

① insurance policy
② insurance certificate
③ open cover
④ insurance premium

<제3과목> 무역실무

51 승낙의 효력발생에 관한 국제물품매매계약에 관한 유엔협약(CISG)의 규정으로 옳지 않은 것은?

① 서신의 경우 승낙기간의 기산일은 지정된 일자 또는 일자의 지정이 없는 경우에는 봉투에 기재된 일자로부터 기산한다.

② 승낙이 승낙기간 내에 청약자에게 도달하지 아니하면 그 효력이 발생하지 아니한다.

③ 구두청약에 대해서는 특별한 사정이 없는 한, 즉시 승낙이 이루어져야 한다.

④ 지연된 승낙의 경우 청약자가 이를 인정한다는 뜻을 피청약자에게 통지하더라도 그 효력이 발생하지 아니한다.

52 다음 무역계약에 대한 설명 중 옳지 않은 것은?

① 협의의 무역계약은 국제물품매매계약이라고 볼 수 있으며 이외의 기타계약을 포함하면 광의의 무역계약이 된다.

② 매도인과 매수인간에 오랜 거래관계를 가지고 있는 경우에는 Case by case contract보다는 Master contract가 바람직하다.

③ 미국의 계약법 리스테이트먼트는 기존판례들을 약술하여 정리한 것이다.

④ 양도승인에 의한 인도에는 점유개정, 간이인도, 목적물 반환청구권의 양도가 있다.

53 신용장 개설 시 유의사항에 대한 설명으로 옳지 않은 것은?

① 수익자, 개설의뢰인의 회사명 등은 약어를 사용하지 않는 것이 좋다.

② 신용장은 명시적으로 'Transferable'이라고 표시된 경우에 한해 양도될 수 있다.

③ 선적기일, 유효기일 및 서류제시기일 표기 시 해석상 오해의 소지가 없도록 월(month) 표시는 문자로 하지 않는 것이 좋다.

④ 신용장 금액 앞에 'about', 'approximately' 또는 이와 유사한 표현이 있는 경우 10% 이내에서 과부족을 인정한다.

54 추심결제방식에 대한 설명으로 옳지 않은 것은?

① 은행을 통해 환어음을 수입상에게 제시하여 대금을 회수한다.

② D/P(Documents against Payment) 방식과 D/A(Documents against Acceptance) 방식이 있다.

③ URC 522(Uniform Rules for Collection 522)이 적용되며 은행은 이에 따라 서류를 심사할 의무를 부담한다.

④ 신용장 거래에 비해 은행수수료가 낮다.

55 EXW 조건과 FCA 조건의 차이를 설명한 것 중 옳은 것은?

	매도인이 운송수단에 적재하여 인도할 의무	매도인의 수출통관 의무
㉠	EXW, FCA	EXW, FCA
㉡	EXW, FCA	FCA
㉢	FCA	EXW, FCA
㉣	FCA	FCA

① ㉠   ② ㉡   ③ ㉢   ④ ㉣

56 신용장의 조건변경 시 유의사항으로 옳지 않은 것은?

① 사소한 분쟁을 사전에 예방하기 위하여 수익자는 조건 변경에 대해 수락하거나 거절한다는 의사표시를 명시적으로 하는 것이 좋다.

② 수익자는 여러 개의 조건변경이 포함된 하나의 조건변경통지서에서의 일부의 조건만 선택적으로 수락할 수 있다.

③ 수익자가 조건변경에 대한 승낙 또는 거절의 통고를 해야 하지만 그런 통고를 하지 않은 경우, 신용장 및 아직 승낙되지 않은 조건변경에 일치하는 제시는 수익자가 그러한 조건변경에 대하여 승낙의 통고를 행하는 것으로 본다.

④ 조건변경을 통지하는 은행은 조건변경을 송부해 온 은행에게 승낙 또는 거절의 모든 통고를 하여야 한다.

57 해상운송장(Sea Waybill)에 대한 설명으로 옳지 못한 것은?

① 해상운송계약을 증빙하는 서류로 운송회사의 화물수령증이라는 점에서 선하증권(B/L)과 같은 기능을 한다.

② 해상운송장(Sea Waybill)이 유통불능이라는 점에서 기명식 선하증권(Straight B/L)과 유사하다.

③ 해상운송장(Sea Waybill)은 제3자 양도가 불가능하다.

④ 수하인이 화물수령을 위해 해상운송장(Sea Waybill) 원본을 운송회사에 제출해야 한다.

58 제3자 개입에 의한 무역클레임 해결방법에 대한 설명으로 옳지 않은 것은?

① 조정안에 대하여 당사자가 수락할 의무는 없으며 어느 일방이 조정안에 불만이 있는 경우에는 조정으로는 분쟁이 해결되지 못한다.

② 알선은 형식적 절차를 거치며, 성공하는 경우 당사자 간에 비밀이 보장되고 거래관계를 계속 유지할 수 있다.

③ 중재는 양 당사자가 계약체결 시나 클레임이 제기된 후에 이 클레임을 중재로 해결할 것을 합의하는 것이 필요하다.

④ 소송은 사법협정이 체결되어 있지 않는 한, 소송에 의한 판결은 외국에서의 승인 및 집행이 보장되지 않는다.

59 신용장의 양도와 관련된 설명으로 옳지 않은 것은?

① 분할양도는 분할선적이 허용된 경우에만 가능하다.

② 양도취급 가능은행은 원신용장에 지급, 인수, 매입은행이 지정된 경우에 그 은행이 양도은행이 된다.

③ 양도는 1회에 한해서만 허용된다.

④ 양수인이 원수익자에게 양도환원(Transfer back)하는 경우는 허용되지 않는다.

60 다음은 청약의 취소(Revocation)와 철회(Withdrawal)에 대한 설명이다. (   ) 안에 들어갈 내용이 옳게 나열된 것은?

(a)가 청약의 효력발생 후 효력을 소멸시키는 반면, (b)는 청약의 효력이 발생되기 전에 그 효력을 중지시키는 것이다. 비록 청약이 (c)이라도 청약의 의사표시가 상대방에 도달하기 전에 또는 도달과 동시에 (d)의 의사표시가 피청약자에게 (e)한/된 때에는 (d)가 가능하다.

① a) 청약의 취소, b) 청약의 철회, c) 취소불능, d) 철회, e) 도달

② a) 청약의 철회, b) 청약의 취소, c) 철회불능, d) 취소, e) 도달

③ a) 청약의 취소, b) 청약의 철회, c) 취소불능, d) 철회, e) 발송

④ a) 청약의 철회, b) 청약의 취소, c) 철회불능, d) 취소, e) 발송

61 환어음의 임의기재사항으로 옳지 않은 것은?

① 환어음의 번호

② 지급인의 명칭

③ 환어음의 발행매수 표시

④ 신용장 또는 계약서 번호

62 우리나라에서 유럽대륙, 스칸디나비아반도 및 중동 간을 연결하는 시베리아횡단철도 복합운송 경로로 옳은 것은?

① SLB

② ALB

③ Mini Land Bridge

④ Interior Point Intermodal

63 신용장통일규칙(UCP 600)에서 규정하고 있는 선하증권의 수리요건으로 볼 수 없는 것은?

① 운송인의 명칭과 운송인, 선장 또는 지정 대리인이 서명한 것

② 화물의 본선적재가 인쇄된 문언으로 명시되어 있거나 본선 적재부기가 있는 것

③ 신용장에 지정된 선적항과 양륙항을 명시한 것

④ 용선계약에 따른다는 명시가 있는 것

64 화물, 화주, 장소를 불문하고 운송거리를 기준으로 일률적으로 운임을 책정하는 방식은?

① Ad Valorem Freight

② Minimum Rate

③ Discrimination Rate

④ Freight All Kinds Rate

65 해상보험에 대한 설명 중 옳지 않은 것은?

① 해상위험은 항해에 기인하거나 항해에 부수하여 발생되는 사고를 말한다.

② 해상손해는 피보험자가 해상위험으로 인해 보험의 목적인 선박, 적하 등에 입는 재산상의 불이익을 말하며 물적손해, 비용손해, 책임손해가 포함된다.

③ 추정전손은 보험목적물을 보험자에게 정당하게 위부함으로써 성립되며, 만약 위부(Abandonment)를 하지 않을 경우 이는 현실전손으로 처리될 수 있다.

④ 적하보험에서 사용되고 있는 ICC(B)와 ICC(C)에서는 열거책임주의 원칙을 택하고 있다.

66 국제팩토링결제에 관한 설명으로 옳지 않은 것은?

① 수출팩터가 전도금융을 제공함으로써 효율적으로 운전자금을 조달할 수 있다.

② 수출자는 대금회수에 대한 위험부담 없이 수입업자와 무신용장 거래를 할 수 있다.

③ 국제팩토링결제는 L/C 및 추심방식에 비해 실무절차가 복잡하다.

④ 팩터가 회계업무를 대행함으로써 수출채권과 관련한 회계장부를 정리해 준다.

67 ICC(C) 조건의 담보위험에 해당되지 않는 것은?

① 공동해손희생

② 화재, 폭발

③ 갑판 유실

④ 육상운송 용구의 전복, 탈선

68 인코텀즈(Incoterms) 2010에 관한 내용 중 옳지 않은 것은?

① FCA의 경우 Buyer가 자신을 위하여 지정된 도착지까지 적하보험에 부보한다.

② CPT의 경우 Buyer가 자신을 위하여 지정된 도착지까지 적하보험에 부보한다.

③ CIP의 경우 Buyer가 자신을 위하여 지정된 도착지까지 적하보험에 부보한다.

④ CIF의 경우 Seller가 Buyer를 위하여 도착항까지 적하보험에 부보한다.

69 최저운임으로 한 건의 화물운송에 적용할 수 있는 가장 적은 운임을 의미하는 것은?

① Minimum Charge

② Normal Rate

③ Quantity Rate

④ Chargeable Weight

70 신용장에서 송장(Invoice)을 요구하는 경우 수리되지 않는 송장(Invoice) 명칭으로 옳은 것은?

① Commercial Invoice

② Final Invoice

③ Proforma Invoice

④ Tax Invoice

71 선하증권의 법적 성질에 대한 설명으로 옳지 않은 것은?

① 선하증권은 실정법에 규정된 법정기재사항을 갖추어야 유효하므로 요식증권이다.

② 선하증권은 화물수령이라는 원인이 있어야 발행하는 것이기 때문에 요인증권이다.

③ 선하증권은 권리의 내용이 증권상의 문언에 의하여 결정되기 때문에 유가증권이다.

④ 선하증권은 배서나 인도에 의하여 권리가 이전되기 때문에 유통증권이다.

72 해상보험의 주요 용어 및 내용에 대한 설명으로 옳지 않은 것은?

① Amount Insured는 보험금액으로 사고 발생 시 보험자가 보상하는 최고 한도액이 된다.

② Insurable Value는 피보험목적물의 평가액이다.

③ Under Insurance는 보험가액보다 보험금액이 적은 경우로 둘 간의 비율에 따라 보상한다.

④ 담보는 명시담보와 묵시담보로 구분되는데 감항성담보는 명시담보에 해당된다.

73 신용장통일규칙(UCP 600) 서류심사의 기준에 대한 설명으로 옳지 않은 것은?

① 은행은 서류의 제시일을 포함하여 최장 5은행영업일 동안 서류를 심사한다.

② 운송서류는 선적일 후 21일보다 늦지 않게 제시되어야 하고 신용장 유효기일 이전에 제시되어야 한다.

③ 일치하는 제시는 신용장, 국제표준은행관행, UCP 600에 따라 제시된 서류를 말한다.

④ 서류 발행자에 대한 내용을 명시하지 않은 채로 운송서류, 보험서류, 또는 상업송장 이외의 서류가 요구된다면 은행은 제시된 대로 수리한다.

74 보험계약의 법적 성질에 대한 내용으로 옳지 않은 것은?

① Bilateral Contact : 보험계약당사자 쌍방이 계약상의 의무를 부담한다.

② Consensual Contract : 당사자 간의 의사표시의 합치만으로 계약이 성립하며 그 의사표시에 특별한 방식이 필요하지 않다.

③ Remunerative Contract : 보험자는 계약상 합의된 방법과 범위에서 피보험자의 손해를 보상할 것을 확약하는 대가로 보험료를 수취한다.

④ Formal Contract : 보험증권이 발행되어야만 해상보험계약이 성립한다는 것으로 보험계약 당사자 간의 정해진 계약방식이 필요하다.

75 국제물품매매계약에 관한 유엔협약(CISG)에 따라 수입상이 계약의무를 위반한 수출상에게 원래 물품을 대체할 대체물의 인도를 청구하려고 한다. 이에 대한 내용으로 옳지 않은 것은?

① 매수인이 매도인의 계약위반에 대해서 대체물을 청구한다면 발생한 손해에 대해서는 배상을 청구할 권리가 없다.

② 매도인의 계약위반이 본질적인 계약위반에 해당할 때에만 매수인이 대체물의 인도를 청구할 수 있다.

③ 매수인이 물품을 수령했으나 계약에 부적합한 인도가 있었고 수령한 상태와 동등한 상태로 물품을 반환할 수 있어야만 매도인은 대체물을 청구할 수 있다.

④ 매수인은 물품이 계약에 부적합하다는 사실에 대해 매도인에게 통지해야 하며 이 통지와 동시에 또는 그 후 합리적인 기간 안에 대체물을 청구해야 한다.

해커스 무역영어 1급 4주 완성 이론+기출문제

[01~02] Read the following and answer the questions.

Dear Sirs,

We received your letter on April 5, in which you asked us to issue immediately a letter of credit (ⓐ) your order No.146.

We have asked today the Korean Exchange Bank in Seoul to issue an irrevocable and confirmed letter of credit in your favor for USD250,000 only, and this credit will be valid until May 20.

This credit will be advised and confirmed by Ⓐ the New York City Bank, N.Y. They will accept your (ⓑ) drawn at 60 days after (ⓒ) under the irrevocable and confirmed L/C.

Please inform us by telex or fax immediately of the (ⓓ) as soon as the goods have been shipped.

Faithfully yours,

01 Choose the wrong role which the underlined Ⓐ does not play.

① confirming bank   ② advising bank

③ issuing bank   ④ accepting bank

02 Select the wrong word in the blanks ⓐ~ⓓ.

① ⓐ covering

② ⓑ draft

③ ⓒ sight

④ ⓓ maturity

03 Which of the following has a different purpose of replying from the others?

We would appreciate it if you would inform us of their financial standing and reputation. Any information provided by you will be treated as strictly confidential, and expenses will be paid by us upon receipt of your bill.

Your prompt reply will be much appreciated.

① The company is respected through the industry.

② Their accounts were not always settled on time.

③ As far as our information goes, they are punctually meeting their commitments.

④ They always meet their obligations to our satisfaction and their latest financial statements show a healthy condition.

04 Which of the following is NOT true about the CPT rule under Incoterms 2020?

① The seller delivers the goods to the carrier or delivers the goods by procuring the goods so delivered.

② The seller contracts for and pay the costs of carriage necessary to bring the goods to the named place of destination.

③ The seller fulfills its obligation to deliver when the goods reach the place of destination.

④ The seller must pay the costs of checking quality, measuring, weighing and counting necessary for delivering the goods.

05 Which of the followings is CORRECT according to the letter received by Mr. Beals below?

> Dear Mr. Beals,
>
> Our Order No.14478.
>
> We are writing to you to complain about the shipment of blue jeans we received on June 20, 2019 against the above order.
>
> The boxes in which the blue jeans were packed were damaged, and looked as if they had been broken in transit. From your invoice No.18871, we estimated that twenty-five blue jeans have been stolen, to the value of $550. Because of the damages in the boxes, some goods were also crushed or stained and cannot be sold as new articles in our shops.
>
> As the sale was on a CFR basis and the forwarding company was your agents, we suggest you contact them with regard to compensation.
>
> You will find a list of the damaged and missing articles enclosed, and the consignment will be put to one side until we receive your instructions.
>
> Your sincerely,
>
> Peter Jang
>
> Encl. a list of the damaged and missing articles

① Mr. Beals will communicate with their forwarding company for compensation.

② Mr. Jang intends to send back the damaged consignment to Mr. Beals.

③ Mr. Beals would receive the damaged consignment.

④ Mr. Jang believes that Mr. Beals sent the damaged article.

06 Which of the following is LEAST likely to be included in a reply?

> Dear Mr. Song,
>
> Thank you for your letter of December 21, making a firm offer for your Ace A/V System. All terms and conditions mentioned in your letter,
>
> including proposed quantity discount scheme, are quite acceptable, and we would like to place an initial order for 200 units of the Ace System.
>
> The enclosed Order Form No. KEPP-2345 gives the particulars concerning this order. For further communication and invoicing, please refer to the above order number.

① Provided you can offer a favorable quotation and guarantee delivery within 6 weeks from receipt of order, we will order on a regular basis.

② Once we have received your L/C, we will process your order and will ship the units as instructed.

③ We are afraid that the product listed in your order has been discontinued since last January this year.

④ As we do not foresee any problem in production and shipment of your order, we expect that this order will reach you on time.

07 Select the right words in the blanks under negotiation letter of credit operation.

> We hereby engage with (   ) that draft(s) drawn under and negotiated in (   ) with terms and conditions of this credit will be duly (   ) presentation.

① drawers and/or drawee - accordance - paid on

② drawers and/or bona fide holders - conformity - honoured on

③ drawers and/or payee - conformity - accepted on

④ drawers and/or bone fide holders - accordance - accepted on

08 Which is right under the following passage under Letter of Credit transaction?

> Where a credit calls for insurance certificate, insurance policy is presented.

① Insurance policy shall accompany a copy of insurance certificate.

② Insurance certificate shall only be presented.

③ Insurance policy can be accepted.

④ Insurance certificate shall accompany a copy of insurance policy.

[09~10] Read the following letter and answer the

> questions.
>
> Dear Mr. Simpson,
>
> Could you please ⓐ pick up a consignment of 20 C2000 computers and make the necessary arrangements for them to be ⓑ shipped to Mr. M. Tanner, NZ Business Machines Pty, 100 South Street, Wellington, New Zealand?
>
> Please ⓒ handle all the shipping formalities and insurance, and send us five copies of the bill of lading, three copies of the commercial invoice, and the insurance certificate. We will ⓓ advise our customers of shipment ourselves.
>
> Could you handle this as soon as possible? Your charges may be invoiced to us in the usual way.
>
> Neil Smith

09 Which can Not be inferred?

① Mr. Simpson is a staff of freight forwarder.

② Neil Smith is a shipping clerk of computer company.

③ Mr. M. Tanner is a consignee.

④ This email is from a shipper to a buyer.

10 Which could not be replaced with the underlined?

① ⓐ collect

② ⓑ transported

③ ⓒ incur

④ ⓓ inform

11 Select the right words in the blanks (A)~(D) under transferable L/C operation.

> ((A)) means a nominated bank that transfers the credit or, in a credit available with any bank, a bank that is specifically authorized by ((B)) to transfer and that transfers the credit. ((C)) may be ((D)).

① (A)Transferring bank - (B)the issuing bank - (C)An issuing bank - (D)a transferring bank

② (A)Transferring bank - (B)the negotiating bank - (C)A negotiating bank - (D)a transferring bank

③ (A)Issuing bank - (B)the transferring bank - (C)A negotiating bank - (D)an Issuing bank

④ (A)Advising bank - (B)the issuing bank - (C)A negotiating bank - (D)a transferring bank

[12~13] Read the following and answer the questions.

> Dear Mrs. Reed,
>
> Thank you for choosing Madam Furnishing. Further to our telephone discussion on your delivery preference for the Melissa table and modification to the table design, kindly review and confirm the terms below as discussed. Your order, which was scheduled for shipping today, has been put on ((A)) to ensure your requirements are incorporated and that you receive your desired furniture. Your desire to change the colour of the table and delivery schedule has been documented and your order ((B)).
>
> Please be informed that:
>
> The Melissa table is commercially available in Black, Brown, and Red. The production of the table in a different colour is considered as a custom order and attracts an additional fee of $20.
>
> Delivery of the Melissa table on Sunday between 12 noon and 3 pm is possible but will attract an additional fee of $10 which is our standard weekend/public holiday delivery fee.

12 Which of the following statements is TRUE about the message above?

① The message is written to confirm customer's requirements.

② The production of the Melissa table in a different colour other than Black, Brown, and Red is not available.

③ Delivery of the table will attract an additional fee of $10.

④ The customer is not desiring to change color of the table and delivery schedule.

13 Select the right words in the blanks (A), (B).

① hold - modified

② document - modified

③ document - cancelled

④ hold - cancelled

14 Which documentary credit enables a beneficiary to obtain pre-shipment financing without impacting his banking facility?

① Transferable

② Red Clause

③ Irrevocable

④ Confirmed irrevocable

[15~16] Read the following letter and answer the questions.

Your order was shipped on 17 April 2018 on the America, will arrive at Liverpool on 27 April.
We have informed your agents, Eddis Jones, who will make ((A)) for the consignment to be sent on to you as soon as they receive the shipping documents for ((B)).
Our bank's agents, Westmorland Bank Ltd, High Street, Nottingham, will ((C)) the documents: shipped clean bill of lading, invoice, and insurance certificate, once you have accepted our bill.

15 Which can NOT be inferred?

① This letter is an advice of shipment to the importer.

② Eddis Jones is a selling agent for the importer.

③ Westmorland Bank Ltd is a collecting bank in importing country.

④ In documentary collection, financial documents are accompanied by commercial documents.

16 Select the right words in the blank (A), (B), (C).

① (A)arrangements, (B)clearance, (C)hand over

② (A)arrangements, (B)transit, (C)hand over

③ (A)promise, (B)clearance, (C)take up

④ (A)promise, (B)transit, (C)take up

17 Select the best translation.

By virtue of B/L clauses, the carrier and its agents are not liable for this incident. Therefore, we regret to repudiate your claim and suggest that you redirect your relevant documents to your underwriters accordingly.

① B/L 약관에 따라서 운송인과 그 대리인은 본 사고에 대해 책임이 없으므로 당사는 귀사의 클레임을 거부하게 되어 유감이고 따라서 귀사의 보험업자에게 귀사의 관련 서류를 다시 보내도록 제안합니다.

② B/L 조항에 따라서 운송인과 그 대리인은 본 사고에 대해 책임이 없으므로 당사는 귀사의 요구를 부인하게 되어 유감이고 따라서 귀사의 보험업자에게 귀사의 관련 서류를 재지시하도록 제안합니다.

③ B/L 조항에 따라서 운송인과 그 대리인은 본 사고에 대해 책임이 없으므로 당사는 귀사의 클레임을 거부하게 되어 유감이고 따라서 귀사의 보험중개업자에게 귀사의 관련 서류를 재지시하도록 제안합니다.

④ B/L 약관에 따라서 운송인과 그 대리인은 본 사고에 대해 책임이 없으므로 당사는 귀사의 클레임을 부인하게 되어 유감이고 따라서 귀사의 보험중개업자에게 귀사의 관련 서류를 다시 보내도록 제안합니다.

18 Select the right words in the blanks (A)~(D).

We have been very satisfied with your handling of our orders, and as our business is growing we expect to place even larger orders with you in the future. As you know we have been working together for more than 2 years now and we will be glad if you can grant us ((A)) facilities with quarterly settlements. This arrangement will save us the inconvenience of making separate payments on ((B)). Banker's and trader's ((C)) can be provided upon your ((D)). We hope to receive your favorable reply soon.

① (A)open-account - (B)invoice - (C)references - (D)request

② (A)open-account - (B)invoice - (C)referees - (D)settlement

③ (A)deferred payment - (B)check - (C)references - (D)settlement

④ (A)deferred payment - (B)check - (C)referees - (D)request

19 Which of the following clauses is NOT appropriate for describing the obligations of the seller and the buyer as for the Dispute Resolution?

① The parties hereto will use their reasonable best efforts to resolve any dispute hereunder through good faith negotiations.

② A party hereto must submit a written notice to any other party to whom such dispute pertains, and any such dispute that cannot be resolved within thirty(30) calendar days of receipt of such notice(or such other period to which the parties may agree) will be submitted to an arbitrator selected by mutual agreement of the parties.

③ The decision of the arbitrator or arbitrators, or of a majority thereof, as the case may be, made in writing will be final and binding upon the parties hereto as to the questions submitted, and the parties will abide by and comply with such decision.

④ If any term or other provision of this Agreement is invalid, illegal or incapable of being enforced by any law or public policy, all other terms and provisions of this Agreement shall nevertheless remain in full force and effect so long as the economic or legal substance of the transactions contemplated hereby is not affected in any manner materially adverse to any party.

[20~21] Read the following and answer the questions.

We were sorry to learn from your letter of 10 January that some of the DVDs supplied to this order were damaged when they reached you.

(1) Replacements for the damaged goods have been sent by parcel post this morning.

(2) It will not be necessary for you to return the damaged goods; they may be destroyed.

(3) Despite the care we take in packing goods, there have recently been several reports of damage.

(4) To avoid further inconvenience and (   ) to customers, as well as expense to ourselves, we are now seeking the advice of a packaging consultant in the hope of improving our methods of handling.

20 Which is suitable for the blank?

① annoyance

② discussions

③ negotiation

④ solution

21 This is a reply to a letter. Which of the following is NOT likely to be found in the previous letter?

① We can only assume that this was due to careless handling at some stage prior to packing.

② We are enclosing a list of the damaged goods and shall be glad if you will replace them.

③ We realize the need to reduce your selling price for the damaged one and readily agree to the special allowance of 10% which you suggest.

④ They have been kept aside in case you need them to support a claim on your suppliers for compensation.

22 Which of the following is the best title for the passage?

> A system used within some conference systems, whereby a shipper is granted a rebate of freight paid over a specified period subject to his having used Conference line vessels exclusively during that period.

① Contract rate system
② Dual rate system
③ Fidelity rebate system
④ Fighting ship

[23~24] Read the followings and answer the questions.

> Thank you for your recent order, No. 234-234-001.
>
> We have received your letter about the $10,000 handling charge that was applied to this shipment. This was indeed an error on our ((A)). We do apply a special handling charge to all orders for ((B)) items such as porcelain birdbaths but somehow that notice was deleted temporarily in the page that described the product. We have ((C)) that error on our Web site.
>
> In the meantime, though, we have placed $10,000 to your credit. We apologize for any inconvenience and hope that we will have the opportunity to serve you again in the near future.

23 Which is LEAST correct about the letter?

① The buyer have ordered brittle items.
② There was a miscommunication about the quality of products.
③ The buyer got the information about the product in the web homepage.
④ For the orders which deal with brittle items, there must be an additional handling charge.

24 Select the right words in the blanks (A), (B), (C).

① part . fragile . corrected
② side . fragile . contemplated
③ part . solid . corrected
④ side . solid . contemplated

25 Which is NOT properly translated into Korean?

> (a) We regret having to remind you that we have not received payment of the balance of £105.67 due on our statement for December.
> (b) This was sent to you on 2 January and a copy is enclosed.
> (c) We must remind you that unusually low prices were quoted to you on the understanding of an early settlement.
> (d) It may well be that non-payment is due to an oversight, and so we ask you to be good enough to send us your cheque within the next few days.

① (a) 12월 계산서에 지급되어야 하는 105.67파운드가 아직 정산되지 않아 독촉장을 보내게 되어 유감입니다.
② (b) 계산서는 1월 2일에 발송하였으며 여기 사본을 동봉합니다.
③ (c) 귀하에게 상기시켜 드리는 이번 건은 유독 낮은 가격을 빨리 견적해 드린 것임을 이해해 주시기 바랍니다.
④ (d) 혹시 실수로 금액 지불이 늦어진 것이라면 2~3일 내로 수표를 보내 주셨으면 감사하겠습니다.

<제2과목> 영작문

26 Which of the following BEST fits the blank (a)~(c)?

> 1. The negotiating bank pays the seller or ((a)) B/E drawn by the seller, and sends the shipping documents to the issuing bank in the buyer's country.
> 2. The issuing bank releases the shipping documents to the buyer in importing country against ((b)).
> 3. The accounter gets the consignment by presenting the ((c)) to the shipping company.

① (a)discounts - (b)payment - (c)shipping documents

② (a)honours - (b)negotiation - (c)bill of lading

③ (a)honours - (b)negotiation - (c)shipping documents

④ (a)discounts - (b)payment - (c)bill of lading

27 Select the one which fits the blanks under the UCP600.

> A nominated bank acting on its nomination, a confirming bank, if any, or the issuing bank may accept a commercial invoice issued for an amount (   ), and its decision will be binding upon all parties, provided the bank in question has not honoured or negotiated for an amount (   ).

① in excess of the amount permitted by the credit - less than that permitted by the credit

② less than the amount permitted by the credit - less than that permitted by the credit

③ less than the amount permitted by the credit - in excess of that permitted by the credit

④ in excess of the amount permitted by the credit - in excess of that permitted by the credit.

28 Select the wrong word in the blank.

① (   ) means a bank, other than the issuing bank, that has discounted or purchased a draft drawn under a letter of credit. (A negotiating bank)

② (   ) issued by a bank in Korea in favour of the domestic supplier is to undertake the bank's payment to the supplier of raw materials or finished goods for exports on behalf of the exporter. (Local L/C)

③ (   ) has a condition that the amount is renewed or automatically reinstated without specific amendments to the credit. (Revolving L/C)

④ Banking charges in relation to L/C are borne by the parties concerned. All banking charges outside importer's country are usually for the account of (   ). (applicant)

29 What is NOT true about the Institute Cargo Clauses?

① Only difference between ICC (B) and ICC (C) is the additional risks covered under ICC (B) cargo insurance policies.

② ICC (B) covers loss of or damage to the subjectmatter insured caused by entry of sea lake or river water into vessel craft hold conveyance container or place of storage but ICC (C) does not.

③ ICC (B) covers loss of or damage to the subjectmatter insured caused by general average sacrifice but ICC (C) does not.

④ ICC (C) is the minimum cover for cargo insurance available in the market.

30 Which of the following words is NOT suitable for the blanks (a)~(d) below?

In all break-bulk and bulk vessels, there is a document called ((a)). This document is like a delivery note and has all the information pertaining to the shipment like cargo description, number of bundles, weight, measurement, etc and this document is handed over to the ship at the time of loading.

If any discrepancies are found between the actual cargo delivered and the ((a)), the Chief Mate will check the cargo and document such discrepancies to confirm that the cargo was received in that condition. This was possible in the era of pre-containerization because the ship/agents were able to physically check and verify the cargo.

However, in the case of containerized cargoes and especially ((b)) cargoes, the carrier/agents are not privy to the packing of the containers and the nature of the cargo. The carrier relies on the information provided by the shipper in terms of the cargo, number of packages, weight and measurement. Hence the clauses ((c)) is put on the ((d)) to protect the carrier from any claims that the shipper might levy on them at a later stage.

① (a) Mate's Receipt
② (b) LCL
③ (c) SHIPPER'S LOAD, STOW, AND COUNT
④ (d) Bill of Lading

31 Which of the following statement on General Average in the marine insurance is NOT correct?

① Defined by York Antwerp Rules 1994 of General Average, these rules lay guidelines for the distribution of loss in an event when cargo has to be jettisoned in order to save the ship, crew, or the remaining cargo.

② A loss is deemed to be considered under general average if and only if the reason of sacrifice is extraordinary or the sacrifice is reasonably made for the purpose of common safety for preserving the property involved.

③ General average shall be applied only for those losses which are linked directly with the material value of the cargo carried or the vessel.

④ Any claims arising due to the delay, a loss or expense caused due to loss of market or any indirect loss must be accounted into general average.

32 Choose the most appropriate term to complete the sentence under UCP600.

The description of the goods in the (   ) must correspond with the description in the credit, and the (   ) must be made out in the name of the Applicant.

① bill of lading   ② commercial invoice
③ sea waybill   ④ bill of exchange

33 Choose one which can NOT replace each underline.

You have been with us for over 20 years. Such loyalty cannot be overlooked. We have looked into your credit account with us and have decided to help. As you are aware, (a) you have four overdue invoices, the latest is about six months overdue. This is unlike you; therefore we have assumed that these (b) delays are connected to the current economic situation your company (c) is going through.

We like to offer you a 20% discount on all the overdue invoices if (d) payment is made within the next 30 days from today. We have attached the new invoices to this email. We believe you place a great value on the credit relationship you have with us. Therefore, we hope to receive the payments at the stipulated date.

① (a) four invoices are still outstanding
② (b) timely payment
③ (c) is encountering
④ (d) the settlement of the invoice is organized

34 Which word fits best for the blank?

> We have already explained that it is essential for medical equipment to arrive (　　) due dates as late delivery could create a very serious problem.

① on 　　　　　② for

③ at 　　　　　④ from

35 Which of the following has different intention from the others?

① Your patience and understanding would be greatly appreciated.

② A short extension would be very helpful to us, as it would give us an extra month to clear the checks.

③ We ask that you grant the extension this one time. We assure you that this will not happen again.

④ We are sorry to hear that the bankruptcies of two of your clients have been causing you difficulties.

36 Select the wrong word in view of document examination.

> When the address and contact details of (　ⓐ　) appear as part of (　ⓑ　) or (　ⓒ　) details, they are not to (　ⓓ　) with those stated in the credit.

① ⓐ the applicant

② ⓑ the consignee

③ ⓒ notify party

④ ⓓ agree

37 Select the wrong word in the blank.

> Documents for which the UCP600 transport articles do not apply are (　　).

① Delivery Note

② Delivery Order

③ Cargo Receipt

④ Multimodal Transport Document

38 Fill in the blanks (a)~(b) with the best word(s).

> To date, no payments have been received from you, and we are assuming that this is merely (a) on your side. Please remit the full (b) _____ due amount immediately.

① (a) an oversight　　(b) past

② (a) an oversight　　(b) intended

③ (a) a fortnight　　(b) intended

④ (a) a fortnight　　(b) past

39 Which of the following sentences is Not correct?

> Dear Mr. Kim,
>
> Thank you for your inquiry on April 13, (a) expressing interest in our software products. In reply to your letter, we are enclosing a detailed catalog and price lists (b) for our design software you required.
>
> (c) Beside those advertising in the Business Monthly, the attached illustrated brochure shows various softwares available for you.
>
> If you have any questions or concerns (d) that are not covered in the materials we sent you, please do not hesitate to contact us at any time.

① (a)　　　　　② (b)

③ (c)　　　　　④ (d)

[40~41] Read the following and answer the questions.

> Dear Mr. MacFee,
>
> We are writing to you on the recommendation of Mr. David Han, Chief Accountant at Hannam Trading. He advised us to contact you as a referee concerning the credit facilities which his company has asked us for.
>
> Could you confirm that the company is sound enough to meet credits of USD3,000,000?
>
> We would be most grateful for a reply (　(A)　).
>
> Yours sincerely,

40 What does the underlined credit facilities imply?

① The potential buyer wants to settle some days later.

② The seller wants to have some loans from bank.

③ The seller wants to have credit from the potential buyer.

④ The potential buyer may ask his bank to open credit.

41 Fill in the blank (A) with suitable word.

① at your earliest convenience

② by the time we arranged

③ at their early convenience

④ to my company's satisfaction

42 Which of the following best fits the blank?

> (   ) are used for taking goods from a port out to a ship, or vice versa. They can also do the same work as a barge.

① Car ferry   ② Oil-tanker

③ Lighters   ④ Trailors

[43~44] Read the following and answer the questions.

> We were surprised to receive your letter of 20 November in which you said you had not received payment for invoice No.1555.
> We instructed our bank, Seoul Bank to ((A)) your account in HSBC London, with USD2,000,000 on 2nd November.
> As our bank statement showed the money had been debited from our account, ((B)) as well. It is possible that your bank has not advised you yet.
>
>   Yours sincerely,

43 Fill in the blank (A).

① credit   ② debit

③ sort out   ④ draw

44 What is best for blank (B)?

① We thought that it was double paid to your account

② We assumed that it had been credited to your account

③ We are certain that payment was in order

④ You may debit our account if you want

45 Which sentence is MOST proper for the blank?

> Thank you for submitting your proposal. (   ), as it is still too early to judge whether or not we will be needing to hire an outside house to take care of the website redesign.

① I accept your proposal

② Perhaps we could work together to make this project happen

③ Please let us know the final result of this bid

④ I'm afraid my response will be delayed

46 Which of the following statements about Stand-by L/C is NOT correct?

> (a)A Stand-by Letter of Credit ('SBLC') can be used as a safety mechanism in a contract for service. (b)A reason for this will be to hedge out risk. In simple terms, (c)it is a guarantee of payment which will be issued by a bank on the behalf of a client and which is perceived as the "payment of last resort". (d)This will usually be avoided upon when there is a failure to fulfill a contractual obligation.

① (a)   ② (b)

③ (c)   ④ (d)

47 **Which is NOT correct when the underlined ones (ⓐ~ⓓ) are replaced with the word(s) given.**

당사는 귀사 앞으로 12월 10일까지 유효한 총액 10,000달러에 대한 취소불능 신용장을 발행하도록 지시했습니다.

→ We have ⓐinstructed our bank to open an irrevocable letter of credit ⓑin your favor ⓒfor the sum of USD10,000 ⓓvalid until December 10.

① ⓐ instructed → arranged with
② ⓑ in your favor → in favor of you
③ ⓒ for the sum of → amounting to
④ ⓓ valid → expired

48 **Which is best for the blank?**

Under UCP 600, terms such as "first class", "well known", "qualified", "independent", "official", "competent" or "local" used to describe the issuer of a document allow (   ).

① any issuer including the beneficiary to issue that document.
② any issuer except the beneficiary to issue that document.
③ certain issuer in the L/C to issue that document.
④ issuer who is not known to the beneficiary to issue that document.

49 **Chose what is NOT correct 1) ~ 3).**

According to CISG provision, the seller may declare the contract avoided;
1) _____
2) _____
3) _____

① If the failure by the buyer to perform any of his obligations under the contract or this Convention amounts to a fundamental breach of contract.
② If the buyer does not, within the additional period of time fixed by the seller, perform his obligation to pay the price.

③ If the buyer does not, within the additional period of time fixed by the buyer, perform his obligation to deliver the goods.
④ If the buyer declares that the buyer will not perform his obligation to pay the price or take delivery of the goods within the period within the additional period of time fixed by the seller.

50 **Which of the following words is NOT appropriate for the blanks below?**

Demurrage and detention is mostly associated with imports although it may happen in the case of exports as well. ((a)) is a charge levied by the shipping line to the importer in cases where they have not taken delivery of the full container and move it out of the port/terminal area for unpacking within the allowed free days. ((b)), on the other hand, is a charge levied by the shipping line to the importer in cases where they have taken the full container for unpacking (let's say within the free days) but have not returned the empty container to the nominated empty depot before the expiry of the free days allowed.

If a customer took the full box out of the port/terminal on the 7th of July which is within the free days (expiring on the 8th of July), but returned the empty container to the line's nominated depot only on the 19th of July. So, the shipping line will be eligible to charge the consignee ((c)) for 11 days from the 9th July (after expiry of free days) till the 19th July at the ((d)) fixed by the line.

① (a) Demurrage
② (b) Detention
③ (c) demurrage
④ (d) commission

<제3과목> 무역실무

51 대금이 물품의 중량에 의하여 지정되는 경우, 의혹이 있을 때 대금은 무엇에 의해 결정되는가?

① 총중량   ② 순중량

③ 순순중량   ④ 정미중량

52 Incoterms 2020의 FOB 조건에 관한 설명 중 옳지 않은 것은?

① 선적항에서 매수인이 지정한 본선에 계약상품을 인도하면 매도인의 인도 의무가 완료된다.

② FOB 조건은 매도인이 물품을 본선 갑판이 아닌 CY에서 인도하는 경우에도 사용한다.

③ FOB 조건은 FAS 조건에 매도인의 본선적재 의무가 추가된 조건이다.

④ 매수인은 자기의 책임과 비용부담으로 운송계약을 체결하고 선박명, 선적기일 등을 매도인에게 통지하여야 한다.

53 국제물품매매계약에 관한 UN협약(CISG, 1980)상 계약위반에 따른 손해배상책임과 면책에 대한 내용으로 옳지 않은 것은?

① 매도인이 매수인으로부터 공급받은 원자재를 이용하여 물품을 제조하여 공급하기로 한 계약에서 원자재의 하자로 인하여 물품이 계약에 불일치하는 경우에는 매도인은 면책된다.

② 계약당사자가 계약체결 시 예견하지 못한 장해가 발생하여 계약의 이행이 불가능해지는 경우에 의무위반 당사자는 면책된다.

③ 면책은 양 당사자가 모두 주장할 수 있으며 모든 의무에 적용이 된다.

④ 계약불이행 당사자는 계약체결 시 예견하지 못한 장해가 존속하는 기간 동안 손해배상책임으로부터 면제되며 그 장해가 제거된다 하더라도 그 당사자의 의무가 부활되는 것은 아니다.

54 내국신용장의 설명으로 옳지 않은 것은?

① 원신용장을 견질로 하여 발행되는 신용장이다.

② local credit이라고 한다.

③ 사용면에서 양도가능신용장과 유사하다.

④ 수입국의 개설은행이 지급확약을 한다.

55 포페이팅(Forfaiting) 거래방식의 설명으로 옳은 것은?

① 포페이터(forfaiter)의 무소구조건부 어음의 할인매입

② 포페이터(forfaiter)의 조건부 지급확약

③ 포페이터(forfaiter)의 무조건부 지급확약

④ 포페이터(forfaiter)의 소구권부 어음의 할인매입

56 다음 내용은 해상운임 관련 부대운임 중 무엇에 대한 설명인가?

> 대부분의 원양항로에서 수출화물이 특정기간에 집중되어 화주들의 선복수요를 충족시키기 위해 선박용선료, 기기확보 비용 등 성수기 비용상승을 보전받기 위해 적용되고 있는 할증료

① Port Congestion Charge

② Peak Season Surcharge

③ Detention Charge

④ Demurrage Charge

57 해상적하보험의 보험기간과 관련된 설명으로 옳지 않은 것은?

① 해상적하보험은 일반적으로 항해보험형태를 취한다.

② 운송약관(transit clause)에 따라 보험기간이 개시된 후 피보험화물이 통상의 운송과정을 벗어나더라도 보험자의 책임은 계속된다.

③ 2009년 협회적하약관(ICC)에서의 보험기간은 1982년 ICC상의 보험기간보다 확장되었다.

④ 보험기간과 보험계약기간은 일치하지 않을 수도 있다.

58 내국신용장과 구매확인서의 비교 설명으로 옳지 않은 것은?

구 분		내국신용장	구매확인서
㉠	관련법규	무역금융관련규정	대외무역법
㉡	개설기관	외국환은행	외국환은행, 전자무역기반사업자
㉢	개설조건	원자재 금융한도	제한 없이 발급
㉣	발행제한	2차까지 개설 가능 (단, 1차 내국신용장이 완제품 내국신용장인 경우에는 차수 제한 없음)	차수 제한 없이 순차적으로 발급 가능

① ㉠   ② ㉡

③ ㉢   ④ ㉣

59 UN국제물품복합운송조약상 복합운송서류의 유통성 조건에 해당되지 않는 것은?

① 지시식 또는 지참인식으로 발행

② 지시식의 경우 배서에 의해 양도

③ 지참인식의 경우 배서에 의해 양도

④ 복본으로 발행되는 경우 원본의 통수를 기재

60 함부르크규칙(Hamburg rules)상 화물인도의 지연에 따른 운송인의 책임으로 옳은 것은?

① 화물운임의 2배 반에 상당하는 금액

② 화물운임의 2배에 상당하는 금액

③ 화물운임의 3배 반에 상당하는 금액

④ 화물운임의 3배에 상당하는 금액

61 협회적하약관(2009) ICC(A),(B),(C) 조건 모두에서 보상하는 손해로 옳지 않은 것은?

① 지진·화산의 분화·낙뢰

② 피난항에서의 화물의 양륙

③ 육상운송용구의 전복·탈선

④ 본선·부선·운송용구의 타물과의 충돌·접촉

62 협회적하약관(2009) ICC(A) 조건에서 보험자의 면책위험으로 옳지 않은 것은?

① 피보험자의 고의적인 위법행위

② 운항자의 지급불능

③ 동맹파업위험

④ 해적행위

63 포괄보험제도를 활용한 해상보험 방법이 아닌 것은?

① Floating Policy

② Open Cover

③ Open Account

④ Open Slip

64 클레임 해결방법 중 하나인 알선(intercession)에 대한 설명으로 옳지 않은 것은?

① 공정한 제3자 기관이 당사자의 일방 또는 쌍방의 의뢰에 의하여 클레임을 해결하는 방법이다.

② 알선은 강제력이 있다.

③ 알선은 중재와는 달리 형식적 절차를 요하지 않는다.

④ ADR에서 타협 다음으로 비용과 시간차원에서 바람직한 해결방법이다.

65 극히 경미한 손상으로 클레임을 제기하기에 무리가 있는 경우나 무역계약 성립 후 시세가 하락하여 수입업자가 손해를 입을 것으로 예상되는 경우에 감가의 구실로 제기 하는 클레임의 종류는?

① 일반적인 클레임

② 계획적 클레임

③ 마켓 클레임

④ 손해배상 클레임

66 중재에 의하여 사법상의 분쟁을 적정, 공평, 신속하게 해결 함을 목적으로 하는 중재법에 관한 설명으로 틀린 것은?

① 법원은 중재법에서 정한 경우를 제외하고는 이 법에 관한 사항에 관여할 수 없다.

② 중재합의는 독립된 합의 또는 계약에 중재조항을 포함 하는 형식으로 할 수 있다.

③ 중재인의 수는 당사자 간의 합의로 정하나, 합의가 없으면 중재인의 수는 5명으로 한다.

④ 중재판정은 양쪽 당사자 간에 법원의 확정판결과 동일한 효력을 가진다.

67 매도인의 계약위반에 따른 매수인의 권리구제수단으로 옳지 않은 것은?

① 물품명세의 확정

② 추가기간의 지정

③ 대체품 인도청구

④ 대금감액청구

68 송금방식의 특징으로 옳지 않은 것은?

① 은행수수료가 저렴하다.

② 어음법의 적용을 받지 않는다.

③ 결제상의 위험을 은행에 전가할 수 있다.

④ 적용되는 국제 규칙이 없다.

69 Incoterms 2020 가격조건 중 그 뒤에 지정목적지 (named place of destination)가 표시되는 조건으로 옳은 것은?

① FOB   ② CFR

③ CIF   ④ CIP

70 곡물류거래에서 선적품질조건에 해당되는 것으로 옳은 것은?

① T.Q.   ② S.D.

③ R.T.   ④ G.M.Q.

71 기술도입계약에 있어 당사자의무에 대한 설명으로 옳지 않은 것은?

① 기술제공자는 기술도입자에게 계약의 존속기간 동안 기술제공의무가 부담된다.

② 기술제공자는 제공하는 기술에 대한 유효성을 보장해야 한다.

③ 기술도입을 위해 독점적 라이센스계약을 체결한 경우, 기술제공자는 제3자의 권리침해를 배제할 의무가 있다.

④ 기술도입자는 계약을 통해 정해진 시기와 방법에 따라서 기술제공자에게 기술료를 제공해야 한다.

72 복합운송인의 책임에 관한 법제도와 책임한도에 대한 설명으로 옳지 않은 것은?

① 이종책임체계(network liability system)는 손해발생 구간이 확인된 경우와 확인되지 않은 경우로 나누어 각각 다른 책임법제를 적용하는 방법이다.

② 복합운송인은 화물의 손해가 복합운송인의 관리 하에 있는 경우에 책임을 져야 하지만 그 결과를 방지하기 위해 모든 조치를 취한 경우는 예외이다.

③ 수화인은 화물의 인도예정일로부터 연속하여 90일 이내에 인도지연의 통지를 하지 않으면 인도 지연으로 인한 손해배상청구권이 상실된다.

④ 화물의 인도일로부터 2년이 경과한 법적 절차나 중재 절차의 개시는 무효이다.

73 관세법의 법적 성격에 대한 설명으로 적절하지 않은 것은?

① 관세법은 행정법의 일종으로 관세의 부과·징수와 통관 절차에 대한 규율을 중심으로 하고 있기 때문에 권력 행위로서 부담적 행정행위가 대부분을 차지한다.

② 관세는 수입되는 물품에 대해 부과된다는 점에서 보통세, 소비행위를 전제로 한다는 점에서 소비세, 다른 조세와 상관없이 과세한다는 점에서 독립세이다.

③ 관세법은 다수의 WTO협정, 세계관세기구(WCO)협약, 특정국과의 협정, 일반적으로 승인된 국제법규가 관세 제도나 관세율로서 반영되어 있다.

④ 관세법은 상품이 국경을 통과하여 이동하는 수출, 수입, 또는 경유하는 과정에서 폭발물 차단, 마약단속 등의 불법적인 차단이라는 점에서 통관절차법적 성격이 있다.

74 eUCP에 대한 설명으로 옳지 않은 것은?

① 준거문언에 따라 UCP의 부칙으로 적용한다.

② eUCP 신용장에 UCP600이 적용된다.

③ eUCP와 UCP600이 상충하는 경우 eUCP가 적용된다.

④ eUCP는 종이서류 상 신용장 개설과 통지에 있어서도 적용된다.

75 Incoterms 2020에 대한 설명으로 부적절한 것은?

① 이전 버전과 같이 운송수단에 따라 2개 그룹으로 나뉜다.

② DAT규칙은 DPU규칙으로 변경되었으나 매도인의 위험과 비용은 DPU규칙에서도 동일하게 적용된다.

③ CPT규칙과 CIP규칙에서 매도인은 목적지에서 양하 의무가 없다.

④ CIF규칙과 CIP규칙에서 매도인의 부보의무는 IC-C(C)에 해당하는 최소부보 의무로 이전 버전과 같이 유지되었다.

<제1과목> 영문해석

01 Followings are the clauses frequently used for a sales contract. Which of the following clauses LEAST represent 'Entire Agreement' between the seller and the buyer?

① This Agreement together with the Plan supersedes any and all other prior understandings and agreements, either oral or in writing, between the parties with respect to the subject matter hereof and constitutes the sole and only agreement between the parties with respect to the said subject matter.

② This Agreement alone fully and completely expresses the agreement of the parties relating to the subject matter hereof. There are no other courses of dealing, understanding, agreements, representations or warranties, written or oral, except as set forth herein.

③ The failure of any party to require the performance of any term or obligation of this Agreement, or the waiver by any party of any breach of this Agreement, shall not prevent any subsequent enforcement of such term or obligation or be deemed a waiver of any subsequent breach.

④ This Agreement is intended by the parties as a final expression of their agreement and intended to be a complete and exclusive statement of the agreement and understanding of the parties hereto in respect of the subject matter contained herein.

02 What is the purpose of the following correspondence?

> Dear Mr. Mike,
>
> We have organized a series of online coaching clinic for middle schools' table tennis coaches this winter. For the virtual training, we would like to provide all registered participants with a tablet PC for interactive real-time communication.
>
> I saw a catalogue with my colleague showing your company's ranges of tablets. We are planning to make an order for more than 1,000 sets at a time. Is there a discount package available for a bulk purchase? I will also like to know the minimum price if we order for 15 or more desktop PCs with webcam.

① Request for Proposal (RFP)
② Request for Quotation (RFQ)
③ Purchase Order
④ Firm Offer

03 Select the wrong explanation of definitions under the UCP 600.

① Advising bank means the bank that advises the credit at the request of the issuing bank.

② Applicant means the party on whose request the credit is issued.

③ Beneficiary means the party in whose favour a credit is issued.

④ Honour means to incur a deferred payment undertaking and pay at maturity if the credit is available by sight payment.

04 Which documentary credit enables a beneficiary to obtain pre-shipment financing without impacting his banking facility?

① Standby L/C
② Red clause L/C
③ Revolving L/C
④ Back-to-back L/C

05 Under the UCP 600, which of the below shipments will be honoured on presentation?

A documentary credit for USD 160,000 calls for instalment ships of fertilizer in February, March, April and May. Each shipment is to be for about 500 tonnes. Shipments were effected as follows:

a. 450 tonnes sent 24 February for value USD 36,000.
b. 550 tonnes sent 12 April for value USD 44,000.
c. 460 tonnes sent 30 April for value USD 36,800.
d. 550 tonnes sent 04 June for value USD 44,000.

① a only   ② a and b only
③ a, b, and c only   ④ none

06 Which of the following statement about a B/L is LEAST correct?

① A straight B/L is a NEGOTIABLE DOCUMENT.
② An order B/L is one of the most popular and common form of bill of lading issued.
③ When a straight bill of lading is issued, the cargo may be released ONLY to the named consignee and upon surrender of at least 1 of the original bills issued.
④ A straight B/L could be used in international transaction between headquarter and branch.

07 Select the best answer suitable for the blank.

Premium means the (A) or sum of money, paid by the (B) to the (C) in return for which the insurer agrees to indemnify the assured in the event of loss from an insured peril. The insurer is not bound to issue a (D) until the premium is paid.

	(A)	(B)	(C)	(D)
①	consideration	assured	insurer	policy
②	consideration	insurer	assured	policy
③	fees	insurer	assured	certificate
④	fees	assured	insured	certificate

08 Select the best answer suitable for the following passage.

Chartering term whereby the charterer of a vessel under voyage charter agrees to pay the costs of loading and discharging the cargo.

① FI
② FO
③ FIO
④ FIOST

09 Select the best answer suitable for the blank under letter of credit operation.

The beneficiary usually (   ) after loading the goods on board to tender documentary drafts to the negotiating bank within expiry date.

① looks for business connection abroad
② dispatches to the importer Trade Circulars including catalogue
③ applies for the issuance of a Letter of Credit
④ prepares shipping documents and draws a draft for negotiation

10 Select the best one which explains well the following passage.

> The shipping documents are surrendered to the consignee by the presenting bank upon acceptance of the time draft. The consignee obtaining possession of the goods is thereby enabled to dispose of them before the actual payment falls due.

① D/A
② D/P
③ Collection
④ Open Account

11 Which of the followings is APPROPRIATE for (A)?

> (A) transaction is a sale where the goods are shipped and delivered before payment is due. This option is the most advantageous for the importer in terms of cash flow and cost, but it is consequently the highest risky option for an exporter. However, the exporter can offer competitive (A) terms while substantially mitigating the risk of non-payment by using one or more of the appropriate trade finance techniques, such as export credit insurance.

① Telegraphic transfer
② Cash with order
③ Open account
④ Letter of credit

12 Followings are the replies to customer complaints. Which of the following is NOT appropriate?

> A. Thank you for taking time out of your busy schedule to write us and express your grievances on how our products and services do not meet up with your expectations.
> B. This is to confirm that I have seen your email. I look forward to receiving my consignment next week as you promised.
> C. However, we can neither receive the return nor refund you as you demanded. This is because of our company's policy. We make refunds only for orders whose complaints are received within two weeks of purchase.
> D. Despite our effort to deliver your order on time using Skynet Express Delivery Service, it's quite unfortunate that we didn't meet up with the time allotted for the delivery of those products.

① A   ② B
③ C   ④ D

13 Select the best answer suitable for the blank.

> We are (A) of being able to send you the (B) by the end of this week. We shall do (C) in our power to see that such an irregularity is not (D).

	(A)	(B)	(C)	(D)
①	convinced	substitute	all	replace
②	convinced	substitution	all	replace
③	confident	substitution	everything	replaced
④	confident	substitute	everything	repeated

14 Which of the following is LEAST correct according to the discourse?

> Lee : Hello, Mr. Jung. Jack Lee speaking.
>
> Jung: Hello, Mr. Lee. I'm with SRG Electronics. And I was hoping to talk to you about our line of electronic parts.
>
> Lee : Oh, yes, I've heard of SRG. How are things going in Korea?
>
> Jung: Good, thanks. In fact, recently there's been a lot of demand for our parts, so we've been very busy.
>
> Lee : Glad to hear that. I'd certainly be interested in your prices.
>
> Jung: Well, I'm going to be in San Francisco next week and wondering if you have time to get together.
>
> Lee : When will you be here?
>
> Jung: Next Wednesday and Thursday. What does your schedule look like?
>
> Lee : Um... Let me check my calendar. Let's see, I have a meeting on Wednesday morning. How about Wednesday afternoon at about two o'clock?
>
> Jung: That is fine.

① Jung works for SRG Electronics.

② Jung and Lee will meet in San Francisco.

③ Jung and Lee already know each other before this phone call.

④ There are few customers in SRG Electronics.

15 Who is doing export credit insurance agencies in Korea?

> In international trade, export credit insurance agencies sometimes act as bridges between the banks and exporters. In emerging economies where the financial sector is yet to be developed, governments often take over the role of the export credit insurance agencies.

① Korea International Trade Association

② K-Sure

③ Kotra

④ Korcham

16 Select the best answer suitable for the blank.

> (   ) letter of credit states : "Credit available with any bank, by negotiation for payment of beneficiary's draft at sight. The L/C is subject to UCP600".

① Irrevocable Open   ② Revocable Open

③ Irrevocable Special   ④ Revocable Special

17 Which of the followings is NOT appropriate for the reply to a claim letter?

① Upon investigation, we have discovered that defective goods sometimes filter despite rigorous inspection before shipment.

② Ten cases of T.V. Set for our order No. 10 per m/s "Chosun" have reached here, but we immensely regret to have to inform you that six units in C/N 10 are different in quality from the specifications of our Order.

③ As a settlement, we have arranged to reship the whole goods by the first ship available, with a special discount of 3% off the invoice amount.

④ After careful investigation, we could not find any errors on our part, because we took every effort to fill your order as evident from the enclosed certificate of packing inspection.

18 Select the right one in regard to the situation.

> Documents presented under an L/C issued by Roori Bank are fully complied. The applicant has already made payment to his bank and then the issuing bank pays the negotiating bank. Some days after, the applicant finds that the goods are not in good quality. He goes to the issuing bank and requests the bank to refund such payment for him.

① Roori Bank has to refund payment to the applicant.

② Roori Bank has to ask for the opinion of the beneficiary.

③ Roori Bank shall ask refund of money to the beneficiary.

④ Roori Bank has no obligation to refund payment.

19 A credit requires an 'invoice' without further definition. Which of the following MUST be considered to be a discrepancy under UCP600?

> A commercial invoice :
> A. that appears to have been issued by the beneficiary.
> B. that is made out in the name of the applicant.
> C. that is made out in the different currency as the credit.
> D. for which the beneficiary did not sign.

① A only
② A+B only
③ C only
④ D only

[20~21] Read the following and answer.

> Thank you for your letter regarding opening an account with our company for trading our goods. Please fill in the enclosed *financial information* form for 3 years and provide us with two or more trade references as well as one bank reference.
> Of course, all information will be kept in strict confidence.
> Thank you very much for your cooperation.
> Your sincerely,

20 Who is likely to be the writer?

① banker
② seller
③ buyer
④ collector

21 What would NOT be included in the financial information?

① cash flow
② profit and loss account
③ balance sheet
④ draft

[22~23] Read the following and answer.

> Dear Peter Park,
> I intend to place a substantial order with you in the next few months.
> As you know, over the past two years I have placed a number of orders with you and settled promptly, so I hope this has established my reputation with your company. Nevertheless, if necessary, I am willing to supply references.
> I would like, if possible, to settle future accounts every three months with payments against quarterly statements.

22 Which is LEAST similar to settled promptly?

① debited per schedule
② paid punctually
③ cleared punctually
④ paid on schedule

23 What can be inferred from the above?

① Peter Park is a buyer.
② The writer wants to place an initial order with the seller.
③ References are to be provided if the buyer is afraid of seller's credit.
④ The seller may send invoices for settlement on a quarterly basis provided that the request is accepted.

24 Choose the awkward one from the following underlined parts.

> I am sorry to inform you that, due to an (A) expected price increase from our manufacturers in USA, (B) we have no option but to raise the prices of all our imported shoes by 4% from 6 May, 2020. However (C) orders received before this date will be invoiced at the present price levels. (D) We sincerely regret the need for the increase.
> However, we know you will understand that this increase is beyond our control.

① (A) ② (B)
③ (C) ④ (D)

25 Choose the right one for the next underlined part.

> Protection and Indemnity (P&I) insurance contained in an ocean marine policy covers:
> _____

① Ordinary loss or damage in the voyage
② Loss of the shipper fees
③ Marine legal liability for third party damages caused by the ship
④ Damage to another vessel caused by collision

<제2과목> 영작문

26 Which of the following words is not suitable for the blank below?

> The more geographic reach your company has, the more important this clause will become. For example, if you're a small local business dealing 100% exclusively with locals, you may not really need a clause telling your customers which law applies. Everyone will expect it to be the law of whatever state that little local business is in.
>
> Now, take a big corporation with customers and offices in numerous countries around the world. If a customer in Korea wants to sue over an issue with the product, would Korean law apply or would the law from any of the other countries take over? Or, what if you're an American business that has customers from Europe.
>
> In both cases, a/an (   ) clause will declare which laws will apply and can keep both companies from having to hire international lawyers.

① controlling law   ② governing law
③ applicable law   ④ proper law

[27 ~ 28] Read the following and answer.

> The most common negotiable document is the bill of lading. The bill of lading is a receipt given by the shipping company to the shipper. A bill of lading serves as a document of title and specifies who is to receive the merchandise at the designated port. In a straight bill of lading, the seller consigns the goods directly to the buyer. This type of bill is usually not desirable in a letter of credit transaction, because (   ).
> With an order bill of lading the shipper can consign the goods to the bank. This method is preferred in letter of credit transactions. The bank maintains control of the merchandise until the buyer pays the documents.

27 What is nature of straight bill of lading?

   ① non-negotiable bill of lading
   ② negotiable bill of lading
   ③ foul bill of lading
   ④ order bill of lading

28 What is best for the blank?

   ① it allows the buyer to obtain possession of the goods directly.
   ② the shipper can consign the goods to the bank.
   ③ the bank maintains control of goods until the buyer pays the documents.
   ④ the bank can releases the bill of lading to the buyer.

29 Which of the followings has a different meaning with others?

   ① We will give you a special discount if you order by May 12.
   ② You will be given a special discount if you take order until May 12.
   ③ If you order on or before May 12, you will get a special discount.
   ④ A special discount is available for your order being received on or before May 12.

30 Which of the following is appropriate for the blank?

In comparison with lawsuit case in a court, arbitration has advantages of the speedy decision, lower costs, nomination of specialized arbitrators, and (   ).

① international effect of judgement
② mandatory publication of arbitral award
③ legal approach by government
④ higher legal stability

31 Which of the following is NOT appropriate for the blank below?

Types of marine insurance can be differentiated as follows:

(A) caters specifically to the marine cargo carried by ship and also pertains to the belongings of a ship's voyagers.

(B) is mostly taken out by the owner of the ship to avoid any loss to the vessel in case of any mishaps occurring.

(C) is that type of marine insurance where compensation is sought to be provided to any liability occurring on account of a ship crashing or colliding and on account of any other induced attacks.

(D) offers and provides protection to merchant vessels' corporations which stand a chance of losing money in the form of freight in case the cargo is lost due to the ship meeting with an accident.

① (A) : voyage insurance
② (B) : hull insurance
③ (C) : liability insurance
④ (D) : freight insurance

32 Which is NOT grammatically correct?

Thank you for your order of February 23, 2020. We are pleased to inform you that (A) your order No.3634 has been loaded on the M/S Ventura, (B) leaving for Busan on March 10, 2020, and (C) arriving at Genoa around April 3, 2020. (D) The packing was carefully carried out according to your instructions, and we are sure that all goods will reach you in good condition.

① (A)   ② (B)
③ (C)   ④ (D)

33 Select the wrong part in the following passage.

(A) Average adjuster is an expert in loss adjustment in marine insurance, particular with regard to hulls and hull interest. (B) He is more particularly concerned with all partial loss adjustments. (C) He is usually appointed to carry out general average adjustments for the shipowner on whom falls the onus to have the adjustment drawn up. (D) His charges and expenses form part of the adjustment.

① (A)   ② (B)
③ (C)   ④ (D)

34 Select the wrong part in the following passage.

(A) Sea Waybill is a transport document for maritime shipment, which serves as prima-facie evidence of the contract of carriage (B) and as a receipt of the goods being transported, and a document of title. (C) To take delivery of the goods, presentation of the sea waybill is not required; (D) generally, the receiver is only required to identify himself, doing so can speed up processing at the port of destination.

35 Which is NOT grammatically correct?

> (A) All disputes, controversies or differences which may raise (B) between the parties out of or in relation to or (C) in connection with contract, for the breach thereof (D) shall be finally settled by arbitration in Seoul.

① (A) ② (B)
③ (C) ④ (D)

36 Which of the following is LEAST correctly written in English?

① 당사는 귀사에게 당사의 늦은 답장에 대해 사과드리고 싶습니다.
 - We would like to apologize you to our late reply.
② 귀사의 담당자는 당사의 어떤 이메일에도 답을 하지 않았습니다.
 - The person in charge at your company did not respond to any of our emails.
③ 귀사의 제안은 다음 회의에서 다루어질 것입니다.
 - Your suggestion will be dealt with at the next meeting.
④ 신상품 라인에 대하여 설명해 주시겠습니까?
 - Would you account for the new product line?

37 Which of the following is LEAST correctly written in English?

① 이 계약서의 조건을 몇 가지 수정하고 싶습니다.
 - I'd like to amend some of the terms of this contract.
② 가격을 원래보다 20달러 더 낮출 수 있을 것 같네요.
 - I think I can lower the price of $20.
③ 계약 기간은 2년입니다.
 - The contract is valid for two years.
④ 3년간 이 소프트웨어 독점 사용권을 제공해 드릴 수 있습니다.
 - We can offer you an exclusive license to this software for three years.

38 Which of the following is LEAST correctly written in English?

① 제품 No.105와 106호의 즉시 선적이 불가능하다면, 제품 No.107과 108호를 대신 보내주십시오.
 - If Nos.105 and 106 are not available for immediate shipment, please send Nos.107 and 108 instead.
② 이 가격이 귀사에게 괜찮다면 우리는 주문양식을 보내드리고자 합니다.
 - If this price is acceptable to you, we would like to send you an order form.
③ 귀사가 제품을 공급해줄 수 없다면, 이유를 알려주시기 바랍니다.
 - If you cannot supply us with the products, please let us have your explanation.
④ 당사의 송장은 주문한 안락의자들을 7월 12일 오후 5시까지 설치해줄 것을 구체적으로 명시하고 있습니다.
 - Our invoice specifically is stated that the armchairs ordering should be furnished until 5:00 p.m. on July 12.

39 Select the best answer suitable for the blank.

> (   ) are taxes assessed for countering the effect of subsidies provided by exporting governments on goods that are exported to other countries.

① Retaliatory duties
② Countervailing duties
③ Dumping duties
④ Anti-dumping duties

[40~41] Read the following and answer.

> As we wrote you previously about the delays in the delivery of your order, the situation is still the same, the trade union strike is on-going. We apologize for this occurrence, but there is not much that we can do to (   ) this, as it is out of our hands. We again apologize and regret the delay in delivery of your order.
> Yours faithfully,

40 What situation is excused in the above letter?

① late payment   ② force majeure

③ non payment   ④ early delivery

41 Fill in the blank with suitable word.

① rectify   ② examine

③ arrange   ④ file

[42~43] Below is part of shipping letter of guarantee.

> Answer to each question.
>
> Whereas (A) you have issued a bill of lading covering the above shipment and the above cargo has been arrived at the above port of discharge, we hereby request you to give delivery of the said cargo to the above mentioned party without presentation of the original bill of lading.
>
> In consideration of your complying with our above request, we hereby agree to *indemnify* you as follows:
>
> Expenses which you may sustain by reason of delivering the cargo in accordance with our request, provided that the undersigned Bank shall be exempt from liability for freight, demurrage or expenses in respect of the contract of carriage.
>
> As soon as the original bill of lading corresponding to the above cargo comes into our possession, we shall surrender the (B) same to you, whereupon our liability hereunder shall cease.

42 Which is the right match for A and B?

① (A) carrier - (B) Letter of Guarantee

② (A) carrier - (B) Bill of Lading

③ (A) buyer - (B) Bill of Lading

④ (A) seller - (B) Letter of Guarantee

43 Which is similar to the word *indemnify*?

① register   ② reimburse

③ recourse   ④ surrender

[44~45] Read the following and answer.

> Blank endorsement is an act that the (A) endorser signs on the back of Bill of Lading (B) with bearing a specific person when a bill of lading is made out (C) to order or shipper's order. The bill of lading then becomes a bearer instrument and the (D) holder can present it to the shipping company to take delivery of the goods.

44 Which is WRONG in the explanation of blank endorsement?

① (A)   ② (B)

③ (C)   ④ (D)

45 What is correct about the bearer?

① Bearer is someone who owns or possesses a B/L.

② Bearer is not able to assign the B/L to others.

③ Bearer is normally bank in negotiable B/L operation.

④ Bearer can not hold the B/L but endorse it to third party for assignment.

[46~47] Read the following and answer.

> All risks is an insurance term to denote the conditions covered by the insurance.
>
> (A) It is to be construed that the insurance covers each and every loss all the times. In cargo insurance, the term embraces all fortuitous losses such as (   ) occurring during transit and (B) the term incorporates a number of excluded perils.
>
> In other words, all risks insurance is a type of property or casualty insurance policy that (C) covers any peril, as long as the contract does not specifically exclude it from coverage. This means that, (D) as long as a peril is not listed as an exclusion, it is covered.

46 Which is NOT suitable in the explanation of all risks insurance?

① (A) ② (B)
③ (C) ④ (D)

47 Which is NOT appropriate for the blank?

① inherent vice
② fire
③ earthquake
④ jettison

[48~49] Read the following and answer.

> Compared to other payment type, the role of banks is substantial in documentary Letter of Credit (L/C) transactions.
> The banks provide additional security for both parties in a trade transaction by playing the role of intermediaries. The banks assure the seller that he would be paid if he provides the necessary documents to the issuing bank through the nominated bank.
> The banks also assure the buyer that their money would not be released unless the shipping documents such as (　　) are presented.

48 What expression is normally stated for nominated bank in L/C?

① available with
② available for
③ available by
④ claims at

49 Which is NOT suitable for the blank?

① packing list
② bill of exchange
③ invoice
④ inspection certificate

50 Fill in the blanks with right words.

> It must be remembered that the Letter of Credit is a contract between the issuing bank and the (　A　), regardless of any intermediary facilitating banks. Therefore, regardless of a place of presentation different from that of the issuing bank as stated on the Letter of Credit, the beneficiary is at liberty to make a (　B　) presentation to the issuing bank and the issuing bank is obliged to honour if the presentation is compliant.

① (A) beneficiary - (B) direct
② (A) applicant   - (B) direct
③ (A) beneficiary - (B) indirect
④ (A) applicant   - (B) indirect

\<제3과목\> 무역실무

51 UN 국제물품매매에 관한 협약(CISG)의 적용 대상인 것은?

① sales of goods bought for personal, family and household use
② sales by auction
③ sales of ships, vessels, hovercraft or aircraft
④ contracts for the supply of goods to be produced

52 계약형태의 진출방식인 국제라이센스(international license)에 대한 설명으로 옳지 않은 것은?

① 해외시장에서 특허나 상표를 보호하는 동시에 크로스라이센스를 통해 상호교환을 기대할 수 있다.
② 노하우가 라이센스의 대상이 되기 위해서는 공공연히 알려진 유용한 경영상의 정보이어야 한다.
③ 현지국에서 외환통제를 실시할 경우, 해외자회사에서 라이센스를 통해서 본국으로 과실송금이 어느 정도 가능하다.
④ 비독점적 라이센스는 기술제공자가 특정인에게 허락한 것과 동일한 내용의 권리를 제3자에게 허락할 수 있는 조건이다.

53 인코텀즈(Incoterms) 2020의 CIF 조건에 대한 설명으로 옳지 않은 것은?

① 매도인이 부담하는 물품의 멸실 또는 손상의 위험은 물품이 선박에 적재된 때 이전된다.

② 물품이 컨테이너터미널에서 운송인에게 교부되는 경우에 사용하기 적절한 규칙은 CIF가 아니라 CIP이다.

③ 매도인은 물품이 제3국을 통과할 때에는 수입관세를 납부하거나 수입통관절차를 수행할 의무가 있다.

④ 매도인은 목적항에 물품이 도착할 때까지 운송 및 보험 비용을 부담하여야 한다.

54 관세법상 외국물품으로 보기 어려운 것은?

① 수출신고 수리된 물품

② 우리나라 선박이 공해에서 채집한 수산물

③ 외국에서 우리나라에 반입된 물품으로서 수입신고 수리 되기 전의 물품

④ 보세구역으로부터 우리나라에 반입된 물품으로서 수입 신고 수리되기 전의 물품

55 한국의 (주)Haiyang은 베트남의 Hochimin Co., Ltd.로 Chemical 제품 15톤을 수출하기로 하였다. 거래조건은 CIP, 결제조건은 sight L/C이다. Hochimin Co., Ltd.가 거래은행을 통하여 발행한 신용장상에 다음과 같은 문구가 있다. 이에 대한 설명으로 옳지 않은 것은?

+Insurance Policy in duplicate issued to Beneficiary's order and blank endorsed for the invoice value plus 10 pct.

① 보험증권의 피보험자란에 (주)Haiyang이 기재된다.

② 보험증권상에 Hochimin Co., Ltd.의 백지배서가 필요하다.

③ 보험부보금액은 송장금액의 110%이다.

④ 보험증권은 총 2부가 발행된다.

56 신용장 양도 시 확인사항으로 옳지 않은 것은?

① 당해 신용장이 양도가능(Transferable) 신용장인지의 여부

② 개설은행이 신용장상에 지급, 인수 또는 매입을 하도록 수권받은 은행인지의 여부

③ 분할양도의 경우 원수출신용장상에 분할선적을 허용하고 있는지의 여부

④ 제시된 원 수출신용장에 의하여 기 취급한 금융이 없는지의 여부

57 신용장의 기능에 대한 설명으로 옳지 않은 것은?

① 개설은행의 지급 확약을 임의로 취소 또는 변경할 수 없으므로 대금회수의 확실성을 높일 수 있다.

② 수출업자는 대금지급에 대한 은행의 약속에 따라 안심 하고 상품을 선적할 수 있다.

③ 수출업자는 신용장을 담보로 하여 대도(T/R)에 의해 수출금융의 혜택을 누릴 수 있다.

④ 수입업자는 선적서류를 통해 계약 물품이 선적기간 및 신용장 유효기간 내에 선적되었는지를 알 수 있다.

58 화물의 형태나 성질에 관계없이 컨테이너 1개당 얼마라는 식으로 운송거리를 기준으로 일률적으로 책정된 운임은?

① ad valorem freight

② minimum all kinds rate

③ freight all kinds rate

④ revenue ton

59 성격이 다른 계약서의 조항을 고르면?

① 품질조건　　　　　　② 수량조건

③ 결제조건　　　　　　④ 중재조건

60 추심결제방식에 대한 설명으로 옳지 않은 것은?

① 환어음의 지급인이 선적서류를 영수함과 동시에 대금을 결제하는 것은 지급도(D/P)방식이다.

② 추심결제는 수출상이 환어음을 발행하여 선적서류를 첨부하여 은행을 통해 송부하는 방식이다.

③ 은행에 추심업무를 위탁하는 자는 지급인(drawee)이다.

④ 'URC'라는 국제규칙이 적용되며 신용장거래와 비교하면 은행수수료 부담이 적다.

61 전자선하증권이 사용될 경우 사용이 감소될 문서는?

① Letter of Indemnity

② Manifest

③ Letter of Guarantee

④ Delivery Order

62 선하증권의 기능에 대한 설명으로 옳지 않은 것은?

① 선하증권은 권리증권의 기능이 있기 때문에 정당한 소지인이 화물인도를 청구할 수 있다.

② 선하증권은 수취증 기능을 하므로 목적지에서 동일한 물품이 인도되어야 한다.

③ 선하증권이 일단 양도되면 그 기재내용은 양수인에 대해 확정적 증거력을 가진다.

④ 선하증권은 운송계약의 추정적 증거가 되며 운송계약서 라고 할 수 있다.

63 항해용선계약에 대한 설명으로 옳지 않은 것은?

① GENCON 1994 서식이 이용되고 있다.

② 선복에 대하여 일괄하여 운임을 결정하는 용선계약을 lumpsum charter라고 한다.

③ 약정된 정박기간 내에 하역을 완료하지 못한 경우에 demurrage가 발생한다.

④ 용선자는 약정된 정박기간을 전부 사용할 수 있도록 하역작업을 수행하는 것이 바람직하다.

64 보험에 대한 설명으로 옳지 않은 것은?

① 일부 보험의 경우 보험금액의 보험가액에 대한 비율로 비례보상한다.

② 초과보험은 초과된 부분에 대해서는 무효이다.

③ 피보험이익은 보험계약 체결 시에 존재하여야 한다.

④ 해상적하보험의 보험가액은 보험기간 중 불변인 것이 원칙이다.

65 청약의 효력이 소멸되는 경우가 아닌 것은?

① 피청약자의 청약거절

② 유효기간 경과

③ 당사자의 사망

④ 청약조건의 조회

66 청약의 유인에 대한 설명으로 옳지 않은 것은?

① 피청약자가 승낙하여도 청약자의 확인이 있어야 계약이 성립한다.

② 청약자는 피청약자의 승낙만으로는 구속되지 않으려는 의도를 가진다.

③ 불특정인, 불특정집단을 대상으로 이루어진다.

④ Sub-con Offer와는 전혀 다른 성격을 지닌다.

67 해상보험에 대한 설명으로 옳지 않은 것은?

① 해상보험은 가입대상에 따라 선박보험과 적하보험으로 나눌 수 있다.

② 해상적하보험은 우리나라 상법상 손해보험에 해당된다.

③ 추정전손은 현실전손이 아니지만 현실적, 경제적으로 구조가 어려운 상태이다.

④ 현실전손인 경우에는 반드시 위부통지를 해야 한다.

68 매도인이 계약을 위반했을 때 매수인의 권리구제 방법으로 볼 수 없는 것은?

① 매도인이 계약을 이행하지 않는 경우에 매수인은 원칙적으로 계약대로의 이행을 청구할 수 있다.

② 매수인은 매도인의 의무이행을 위하여 합리적인 추가기간을 지정할 수 있다.

③ 계약상 매도인이 합의된 기일 내에 물품의 명세를 확정 하지 아니한 때에는 매수인이 물품 명세를 확정할 수 있다.

④ 물품이 계약에 부적합한 경우에 모든 상황에 비추어 불합리하지 않는 한, 매수인은 매도인에 대하여 하자 보완을 청구할 수 있다.

69 우리나라 중재법상 임시적 처분의 주요 내용으로 옳지 않은 것은?

① 분쟁의 해결에 관련성과 중요성이 있는 증거의 보전

② 본안(本案)에 대한 중재판정이 있을 때까지 현상의 유지 또는 복원

③ 중재판정의 집행 대상이 되는 부채에 대한 보전 방법의 제공

④ 중재절차 자체에 대한 현존하거나 급박한 위험이나 영향을 방지하는 조치 또는 그러한 위험이나 영향을 줄 수 있는 조치의 금지

70 비용의 분기가 선적지에서 이뤄지는 Incoterms 2020 조건으로 옳은 것은?

① FOB   ② DAP

③ DDP   ④ CIF

71 중재계약에 대한 설명으로 옳지 않은 것은?

① 중재조항은 직소금지의 효력이 있다.

② 중재계약은 주된 계약에 대하여 독립성을 갖는다.

③ 중재계약에는 계약자유의 원칙이 적용되지 않는다.

④ 중재는 단심제이다.

72 대리점의 권한과 관련 본인으로부터 권한을 부여받지는 못하였으나 법률의 규정에 의하여 본인의 동의 여부를 불문하고 대리점이 권한을 소유하는 것을 무슨 권한이라고 하는가?

① actual authority

② apparent authority

③ presumed authority

④ doctrine of ratification

73 신용장 조건 점검 시 성격이 다른 하나는?

① 검사증명서에 공식검사기관이 아닌 자의 서명을 요구하는 경우

② 화주의 책임과 계량이 표시된 운송서류는 수리되지 않는다는 조건

③ 개설의뢰인의 수입승인을 신용장 유효조건으로 하는 경우

④ 매매계약의 내용과 불일치한 조건이 있는지의 여부

74 전자무역에 대한 설명으로 옳지 않은 것은?

① 무역의 일부 또는 전부가 전자무역문서로 처리되는 거래를 말한다.

② 전자무역은 글로벌B2C이다.

③ 신용장에서 전자서류가 이용될 때 eUCP가 적용될 수 있다.

④ 선하증권의 위기를 해결하기 위해 CMI에서 해상운송장과 전자선하증권에 관한 규칙을 각각 제정하였다.

75 다음은 일반거래조건협정서의 어느 조건에 해당하는가?

> All the goods sold shall be shipped within the time stipulated in each contract. The date of bills of lading shall be taken as a conclusive proof of the date of shipment. Unless specially arranged, the port of shipment shall be at Seller's option.

① 품질조건

② 선적조건

③ 정형거래조건

④ 수량조건

<제1과목> 영문해석

01 What can you infer from the sentence below?

> Trade finance generally refers to export financing which is normally self-liquidating.

① All export amounts are to be paid, and then applied to extend the loan. The remainder is credited to the importer's account.

② Pre-shipment finance is paid off by general working capital loans.

③ Export financing is a bit difficult to use over general working capital loans.

④ All export amounts are to be collected, and then applied to payoff the loan. The remainder is credited to the exporter's account.

02 Below is about del credere agent. Which is NOT in line with others?

> (A) An agreement by which a factor, when he sells goods on consignment, for an additional commission (called a del credere commission), (B) guaranties the solvency of the purchaser and his performance of the contract. Such a factor is called a del credere agent. (C) He is a mere surety, liable to his principal only in case the purchaser makes default. (D) Agent who is obligated to indemnify his principal in event of loss to principal as result of credit extended by agent to third party.

① (A)   ② (B)   ③ (C)   ④ (D)

[03 ~ 04] Read the following and answer.

> We are pleased to state that KAsia in your letter of 25th May is a small but well-known and highly respectable firm, (A) who has established in this town for more than five years. We ourselves have now been doing business with them (B) for more than five years on quarterly open account terms and although (C) they have not taken advantage of cash discounts, they have always paid promptly on the net dates. The credit we have allowed the firm (D) has been well above USD100,000 you mentioned.

03 Who might be the writer?

① Bank   ② Referee

③ Seller   ④ Buyer

04 Which is grammatically WRONG?

① (A)   ② (B)   ③ (C)   ④ (D)

05 Which of the following CANNOT be inferred from the passage below?

Dear Mr. Cooper,

Thank you for your letter in reply to our advertisement in EduCare.

Although we are interested in your proposition, the 5% commission you quoted on the invoice values is higher than we are willing to pay. However, the other terms quoted in your quotation would suit us.

Again we do not envisage paying more than 3% commission on net invoice values, and if you are willing to accept this rate, we would sign a one-year contract with effect from 1 August.

One more thing we would like to add is that the volume of business would make it worth accepting our offer.

Yours sincerely,

Peter

① Peter is an agent.
② Cooper is engaged in a commission based business.
③ 3% commission is a maximum to the Principal to go with.
④ Low commission might be compensated by large volume of business.

06 Select the wrong explanation of negotiation under UCP 600.

(A) Negotiation means the purchase by the nominated bank of drafts (drawn on a bank other than the nominated bank) (B) and/or documents under a complying presentation, (C) by advancing or agreeing to advance funds to the beneficiary (D) on or before the banking day on which reimbursement is due to the issuing bank.

① (A)　　② (B)　　③ (C)　　④ (D)

07 What is correct about the bearer in bill of lading operation?

① Bearer is someone who owns or possesses a B/L.
② Bearer is not able to assign the B/L to other.
③ Bearer is normally second consignor in negotiable B/L operation.
④ Bearer can not hold the B/L but endorse it to third party for assignment.

08 Select the wrong explanation of credit under UCP 600.

(A) Credit means any arrangement, (B) however named or described, (C) that is irrevocable or revocable and thereby constitutes a definite undertaking of (D) the issuing bank to honour a complying presentation.

① (A)　　② (B)　　③ (C)　　④ (D)

09 Select the best answer suitable for the blanks.

Excepted perils mean the perils exempting the insurer from liability where the loss of or damage to the subject-matter insured arises from certain causes such as (A) of the assured, delay, (B), inherent vice and vermin or where loss is not (C) by perils insured against.

① (A) wilful misconduct　(B) ordinary wear and tear　(C) proximately caused
② (A) wilful misconduct　(B) wear and tear (C) proximately caused
③ (A) misconduct　(B) wear and tear　(C) caused
④ (A) misconduct　(B) ordinary wear and tear　(C) caused

10 What is the subject of the passage below?

A written statement usually issued by the issuing bank at the request of an importer so as to take delivery of goods from a shipping company before the importer obtains B/L.

① Letter of Guarantee

② Letter of Surrender

③ Bill of Exchange

④ Trust Receipt

11 Which of the followings is NOT suitable for the blanks below?

A factor is a bank or specialized financial firm that performs financing through the purchase of (A). In export factoring, the factor purchases the exporter's (B) foreign accounts receivable for cash at a discount from the face value, generally (C). It sometimes offers up to 100% protection against the foreign buyer's inability to pay‑with (D).

① (A) account receivables

② (B) long-term

③ (C) without recourse

④ (D) no deductible scheme or risk-sharing

[12~13] Read the following letter and answer the questions.

Thank you for your advice of 15 May. We have now effected (A) to our customers in New Zealand and enclose the (B) you asked for and our draft for £23,100 which includes your (C). Will you please honour the (D) and remit the (E) to our account at the Mainland Bank, Oxford Street, London W1A 1AA.

12 Select the wrong one in the blank (C)?

① discount

② commission

③ charges

④ proceeds

13 Which of the following BEST completes the blanks (A), (B), (D) and (E)?

① (A) dispatch　　　　(B) transport documents
　 (D) documentary draft (E) proceed

② (A) shipment　　　　(B) transport documents
　 (D) clean draft　　　(E) proceed

③ (A) shipment　　　　(B) shipping documents
　 (D) documentary draft(E) proceeds

④ (A) dispatch　　　　(B) shipping documents
　 (D) clean draft　　　(E) proceeds

14 Please put the following sentences in order.

(A) After having dealt with you for many years, I deserve better treatment.

(B) Your competitors will be happy to honor my credit, and I will transfer my future business elsewhere.

(C) I did not appreciate the curt letter I received from your Credit Department yesterday regarding the above invoice, a copy of which is attached.

(D) I've been disputing these charges for two months.

① (C) - (D) - (A) - (B)

② (A) - (B) - (D) - (C)

③ (B) - (D) - (C) - (A)

④ (D) - (A) - (B) - (C)

15 Select the different purpose among the following things.

① The finish is not good and the gilt comes off partly.

② By some mistake the goods have been wrongly delivered.

③ When comparing the goods received with the sample, we find that the color is not the same.

④ All marks must be same as those of invoice in accordance with our direction.

[16~19] Read the following passage and answer.

The UCP 600 definition of complying presentation means a presentation that is in accordance with the terms and conditions of the documentary credit, the applicable provisions of these rules and international standard banking practice.

This definition includes three concepts. First, (A) Second, the presentation of documents must comply with the rules contained in UCP 600 that are applicable to the transaction, i.e., (B). Third, the presentation of documents must comply with international standard banking practice. The first two conditions are determined by looking at the specific terms and conditions of the documentary credit and the rules themselves. ⓐ The third, international standard banking practice, reflects the fact that the documentary credit and ⓑ the rules only imply some of the processes that banks undertake in the examination of documents and in the determination of compliance. ⓒ International standard banking practice includes practices that banks regularly undertake in determining the compliance of documents. ⓓ Many of these practices are contained in the ICC's publication International Standard Banking Practice for the Examination of Documents under Documentary Credits ("ISBP") (ICC Publication No. 681); however, the practices are broader than what is stated in this publication. Whilst the ISBP publication includes many banking practices, there are others that are also commonly used in documentary credit transaction beyond those related to the examination of documents. For this reason, (C).

16 Select the suitable one in the blank (A).

① the presentation of documents must comply with the terms and conditions of the documentary credit.

② the presentation of documents must represent the goods.

③ the passing of the documents by the beneficiary to the issuing bank must be punctual.

④ the presentation of complying documents must made to the nominated banks under the documentary credit.

17 Select the wrong one for the underlined parts.

① ⓐ   ② ⓑ   ③ ⓒ   ④ ⓓ

18 Select the best one in the blank (B).

① those that have been modified or excluded by the terms and conditions of the documentary credit

② those that can not be applied by way of special conditions that exclude the rules

③ those that can not be applied by way of special conditions that modify or exclude the rules

④ those that have not been modified or excluded by the terms and conditions of the documentary credit

19 Select the best one in the blank (C).

① the definition of complying presentation specifically refers to the International Standard Banking Practice publication

② the definition of complying presentation does not specifically refer to the International Standard Banking Practice and UCP publications

③ the definition of complying presentation does not specifically refer to the International Standard Banking Practice publication

④ the definition of complying presentation specifically refers to the International Standard Banking Practice and UCP publications

20 Which is right pair of words for the blanks?

A sight draft is used when the exporter wishes to retain title to the shipment until it reaches its destination and payment is made.

In actual practice, the ocean bill of lading is endorsed by the (A) and sent via the exporter's bank to the buyer's bank. It is accompanied by the draft, shipping documents, and other documents that are specified by the (B). The foreign bank notifies the buyer when it has received these documents. As soon as the draft is paid, the foreign bank hands over the bill of lading with other documents thereby enabling the (C) to take delivery of the goods.

	(A)	(B)	(C)
①	exporter	buyer	buyer
②	exporter	exporter	buyer
③	buyer	exporter	buyer
④	buyer	buyer	buyer

21 Which is NOT suitable in the blank?

The Incoterms® 2020 rules do NOT deal with ( ).

① whether there is a contract of sale at all
② the specifications of the goods sold
③ the effect of sanctions
④ export/import clearance and assistance

22 Which of the following is the LEAST appropriate Korean translation?

① We are very sorry to have to inform you that your latest delivery is not up to your usual standard.
→ 귀사의 최근 발송품은 평소의 수준에 미치지 못하는 것이었음을 알려드리게 되어 유감입니다.

② We must apologize once again for the last minute problems caused by a clerical error on our side.
→ 당사 측의 사소한 실수로 인해 발생한 문제에 대해 마지막으로 다시 사과드려야 하겠습니다.

③ In consequence we are compelled to ask our agents to bear a part of the loss.
→ 따라서 당사는 당사 대리점들이 이번 손실의 일부를 부담해줄 것을 요청하지 않을 수 없습니다.

④ Thank you for your quotation for the supply of ABC but we have been obliged to place our order elsewhere in this instance.
→ ABC의 공급에 대한 견적을 보내주셔서 감사합니다. 하지만 이번에 한해서는 타사에 주문할 수밖에 없게 되었습니다.

23 The following is on Incoterms® 2020. Select the right ones in the blanks.

The Incoterms® rules explain a set of (A) of the most commonly-used three-letter trade terms, e.g. CIF, DAP, etc., reflecting (B) practice in contracts for the (C) of goods.

① (A) twelve (B) business-to-consumer
  (C) sale and purchase
② (A) eleven (B) business-to-business
  (C) sale and purchase
③ (A) eleven (B) business-to-consumer (C) sales
④ (A) twelve (B) business-to-business (C) sales

24 Select the wrong explanation of changes in Incoterms® 2020.

① Bills of lading with an on-board notation could be required under the FCA Incoterms rule.

② Obligations which are listed in one clause.

③ Different levels of insurance cover in CIF and CIP.

④ Arranging for carriage with seller's or buyer's own means of transport in FCA, DAP, DPU and DDP.

25 Select the term or terms which the following passage does not apply to.

> The named place indicates where the goods are "delivered", i.e. where risk transfers from seller to buyer.

① E-term   ② F-terms

③ C-terms   ④ D-terms

<제2과목> 영작문

[26~28] Please read the following letter and answer each question.

(A) We have instructed our bank, Korea Exchange Bank, Seoul to open an irrevocable letter of credit for USD22,000.00 (twenty two thousand US dollars) to cover the shipment (CIF London). The credit is (a) until 10 June 2020.

(B) Bill of Lading (3 copies) Invoice CIF London (2 copies) AR Insurance Policy for USD24,000.00 (twenty four thousand US dollars)

(C) We are placing the attached order for 12 (twelve) C3001 computers in your proforma invoice No.548.

(D) You will receive confirmation from our bank's agents, HSBC London, and you can draw on them at 60 (sixty) days after sight for the full amount of invoice. When submitting our draft, please enclose the following documents.

Please fax or email us as soon as you have arranged (b).

26 Put the sentences (A)~(D) in the correct order.

① (D) - (B) - (A) - (C)

② (C) - (A) - (D) - (B)

③ (D) - (C) - (B) - (A)

④ (B) - (A) - (C) - (D)

27 Which word is Not suitable for (a)?

① invalid   ② in force

③ effective   ④ available

28 Which word is most suitable for (b)?

① shipment   ② insurance

③ negotiation   ④ invoice

29 Select the right term for the following passage.

> The freight is calculated on the ship's space or voyage rather than on the weight or measurement.

① Lumpsum Freight
② Dead Freight
③ Bulky Freight
④ FAK

30 Choose the one which has same meaning for the underlined part under UCP 600.

> We intend to ship a consignment of (A) dinghies and their equipment to London at (B) the beginning of next month under the letter of credit.

① (A) boats - (B) the 1st to the 10th
② (A) yachts - (B) the 1st to the 15th
③ (A) machines - (B) the 1st to the 10th
④ (A) hull - (B) the 1st to the 15th

31 What kind of draft is required and fill in the blank with suitable word?

> This credit is available by draft at sight drawn on us for (   )

① usance - invoice value plus 10%
② demand - the full invoice value
③ demand - invoice value plus 10%
④ usance - the full invoice value

32 Select the wrong part in the following passage.

> (A) Authority to Pay is not a letter of credit, (B) but merely an advice of the place of payment and also specifies documents needed to obtain payment. (C) It obliges any bank to pay. (D) It is much less expensive than a letter of credit and has been largely superseded by documents against payment.

① (A)   ② (B)   ③ (C)   ④ (D)

33 Which of the following is MOST appropriate in the blanks ?

> If a credit prohibits partial shipments and more than one air transport document is presented covering dispatch from one or more airports of departure, such documents are (A), provided that they cover the dispatch of goods on the same aircraft and same flight and are destined for the same airport of destination. In the event that more than one air transport document is presented incorporating different dates of shipment, (B) of these dates of shipment will be taken for the calculation of any presentation period.

① (A) unacceptable - (B) the latest
② (A) unacceptable - (B) the earliest
③ (A) acceptable - (B) the latest
④ (A) acceptable - (B) the earliest

34 Select the best one in the blank.

> If a nominated bank determines that a presentation is complying and forwards the documents to the issuing bank or confirming bank, whether or not the nominated bank has honoured or negotiated, and issuing bank or confirming bank must (   ) that nominated bank, even when the documents have been lost in transit between the nominated bank and the issuing bank or confirming bank, or between the confirming bank and the issuing bank.

① reimburse
② honour or reimburse
③ negotiate or reimburse
④ honour or negotiate, or reimburse

35 A letter of credit requires to present bill of lading and insurance certificate. If the shipment date of bill of lading is 20 May, 2020, which of following document can be matched with such bill of lading?

> A. An insurance certificate showing date of issue as 20 May, 2020
>
> B. An insurance certificate showing date of issue as 21 May, 2020
>
> C. An insurance policy showing date of issue as 20 May, 2020
>
> D. A cover note showing date of issue as 20 May, 2020

① A only
② C only
③ A and C only
④ all of the above

36 Which of the followings is NOT correctly explaining the Charter Party Bill of Lading under UCP 600?

① The charter party B/L must appear to be signed by the master, the owner, or the charterer or their agent.

② The charter party B/L must indicate that the goods have been shipped on board at the port of loading stated in the credit by pre-printed wording, or an on board notation.

③ The date of issuance of the charter party bill of lading will be deemed to be the date of shipment unless the charter party bill of lading contains an on board notation indicating the date of shipment.

④ A bank will examine charter party contracts if they are required to be presented by the terms of the credit.

37 Select the right terms in the blanks?

> Payments under (A) are made direct between seller and buyer whereas those under (B) are made against presentation of documentary bills without bank's obligation to pay.

① (A) Documentary Collection - (B) Letter of Credit
② (A) Remittance - (B) Documentary Collection
③ (A) Letter of Credit - (B) Documentary Collection
④ (A) Remittance - (B) Letter of Credit

38 Which of the following is LEAST correct about the difference between Bank Guarantee and Letter of Credit?

① The critical difference between LC and guarantees lie in the way financial instruments are used.

② Merchants involved in exports and imports of goods on a regular basis choose LC to ensure delivery and payments.

③ Contractors bidding for infrastructure projects prove their financial credibility through guarantees.

④ In LC, the payment obligation is dependent of the underlying contract of sale.

39 Which of the followings is NOT APPROPRIATE as part of the reply to the letter below?

> Thank you for your fax of July 5, requesting an offer on our mattress. We offer you firm subject to your acceptance reaching us by July 20.
>
> Our terms and conditions are as follows :
>
> Items : mattress (queen size)
>
> Quantity : 300 units
>
> Price : USD1,100.00 per unit, CIF New York
>
> Shipment : During May
>
> Payment : Draft at sight under an Irrevocable L/C

① We need the goods in early June, so we want to change only shipment term.

② Thank you for your firm offer, and we are pleased to accept your offer as specified in our Purchase Note enclosed.

③ Thank you for your letter requesting us to make an offer, and we would like to make an offer.

④ We regret to say that we are not able to accept your offer because of high price comparing with that of your competitor.

40 Put the sentences A~D in the correct order?

(A) Finally, in accordance with the instructions of our buyer, we have opened an insurance account with the AAA Insurance Company on W.A. including War Risk.

(B) We enclose a check for $50.00 from Citibank in payment of the premium.

(C) As you know, our buyer directed us to make a marine insurance contract on W.A. including War Risk with you on 300 boxes of our Glasses Frames, which we are shipping to New York by the S.S. "Ahra" scheduled to leave Busan on the 15th February.

(D) We want you to cover us on W.A. including War Risk, for the amount of $2,050.00 at the rate you suggested to us on the phone yesterday, and one copy of our invoice is enclosed herein.

① A - B - C - D
② C - D - B - A
③ D - B - C - A
④ B - C - D - A

41 Where a bill of lading is tendered under a letter of credit, which is LEAST appropriate?

The bill of lading is usually (A) drawn in sets of three negotiable copies, and goods are deliverable against (B) any one of the copies surrendered to the shipping company. The number of negotiable copies prepared would be mentioned on the bill which would also provide that "(C) one of the copies of the bill being accomplished, the others to stand valid". It is, therefore, essential that (D) the bank obtains all the copies of the bill of lading.

① (A)　　② (B)　　③ (C)　　④ (D)

42 What does the following refer to under marine insurance operation?

After the insured gets the claim money, the insurer steps into the shoes of insured. After making the payment of insurance claim, the insurer becomes the owner of subject matter.

① Principle of Subrogation
② Principle of Contribution
③ Principle of Abandonment
④ Principle of Insurable Interest

43 Which of the followings is NOT correctly explaining the arbitration?

① With arbitration clause in their contract, the parties opt for a private dispute resolution procedure instead of going to court.

② The arbitration can only take place if both parties have agreed to it.

③ In contrast to mediation, a party can unilaterally withdraw from arbitration.

④ In choosing arbitration, parties are able to choose such important elements as the applicable law, language and venue of the arbitration. This allows them to ensure that no party may enjoy a home court advantage.

44 Select the right term for the following passage.

> A principle whereby all parties to an adventure, who benefit from the sacrifice or expenditure, must contribute to make good the amount sacrificed or the expenditure incurred.

① General average
② Jettison
③ Particular charges
④ Particular average

45 Select the wrong term in view of the following passage.

> A negotiation credit under which negotiation is not restricted to one nominated bank or which is available through any bank.

① general L/C
② unrestricted L/C
③ open L/C
④ freely acceptable L/C

46 The following are on CIF under Incoterms® 2020. Select the wrong one.

① The insurance shall cover, at a minimum, the price provided in the contract plus 10% (ie 110%) and shall be in the currency of the carriage contract.
② The insurance shall cover the goods from the point of delivery set out in this rule to at least the named port of destination.
③ The seller must provide the buyer with the insurance policy or certificate or any other evidence of insurance cover.
④ Moreover, the seller must provide the buyer, at the buyer's request, risk and cost, with information that the buyer needs to procure any additional insurance.

47 Select the wrong part in the following passage under UCP600.

> (A) Letter of Credit means an engagement by a bank or other person made at the request of a customer (B) that the issuer will honor drafts or other demands for payment upon compliance with the conditions specified in the credit. (C) A credit must be irrevocable. (D) The engagement may be either an agreement to honor or a statement that the applicant or other person is authorized to honor.

① (A)　　② (B)　　③ (C)　　④ (D)

48 Select the wrong one in the blank under Incoterms® 2020.

> The seller must pay (　　　) under FCA.

① all costs relating to the goods until they have been delivered in accordance with this rule other than those payable by the buyer under this rule
② the costs of providing the transport document to the buyer under this rule that the goods have been delivered
③ where applicable, duties, taxes and any other costs related to export clearance under this rule
④ the buyer for all costs and charges related to providing assistance in obtaining documents and information in accordance with this rule

49 The following are the purpose of the text of the introduction of Incoterms® 2020. Select the wrong one.

① to explain what the Incoterms® 2020 rules do and do NOT do and how they are best incorporated
② to set out the important fundamentals of the Incoterms rules such as the basic roles and responsibilities of seller and buyer, delivery, risk etc.
③ to explain how best to choose the right Incoterms rules for the general sale contract
④ to set out the central changes between Incoterms® 2010 and Incoterms® 2020

50 Which of the following is logically INCORRECT?

① A person authorized by another to act for him is called as principal.

② Co-agent means one who shares authority to act for the principal with another agent and who is so authorized by the principal.

③ Agents employed for the sale of goods or merchandise are called mercantile agents.

④ Del credere agent is an agent who sell on behalf of a commission and undertakes that orders passed to the principal will be paid.

<제3과목> 무역실무

51 다음 DPU 조건에 대한 설명 중 틀린 것을 고르시오.

① 매도인은 지정목적지까지 또는 있는 경우 지정목적지에서의 합의된 지점까지 물품의 운송을 위해 자신의 비용으로 계약을 체결하거나 준비하여야 한다.

② 매도인은 목적지까지 운송을 위해 어떠한 운송 관련 보안요건을 준수하여야 한다.

③ 매도인은 자신의 비용으로 매수인이 물품을 인수할 수 있도록 하기 위해 요구되는 서류를 제공하여야 한다.

④ 매도인은 수출통관절차, 수출허가, 수출을 위한 보안통관, 선적전 검사, 제3국 통과 및 수입을 위한 통관절차를 수행하여야 한다.

52 다음 중 권리침해조항의 설명으로 틀린 것을 고르시오.

① 특허권, 실용신안권, 디자인권, 상표권 등의 지적재산권의 침해와 관련된 조항이다.

② 매도인의 면책내용을 규정하고 있고 매수인의 주문내용에 따른 이행에 한정된다.

③ 매수인은 제3자로부터 지적재산권 침해를 받았다는 이유로 매도인에게 클레임을 제기할 수 있다.

④ 선진국으로 수출되는 물품을 주문받았을 경우 특히 이 조항을 삽입해야 한다.

53 다음 인코텀즈(Incoterms) 2020에 대한 설명으로 적절하지 않은 것을 고르시오.

① CIF 조건에서는 협회적하약관 C약관의 원칙을 계속 유지하였다.

② 물품이 FCA 조건으로 매매되고 해상운송 되는 경우에 매수인은 본선적재표기가 있는 선하증권을 요청할 수 없다.

③ 인코텀즈 2020 규칙에서는 물품이 매도인으로부터 매수인 에게 운송될 때 상황에 따라 운송인이 개입되지 않을 수도 있다.

④ 매도인이 컨테이너화물을 선적 전에 운송인에게 교부함으로써 매수인에게 인도하는 경우에 매도인은 FOB 조건 대신에 FCA 조건으로 매매하는 것이 좋다.

54 다음 중 매입은행과 개설은행의 서류 심사와 관련된 내용으로 옳지 않은 것을 고르시오.

① 은행의 서류심사와 수리여부 결정은 선적서류를 영수한 익일로부터 제7영업일이내에 이루어져야 한다.

② 신용장조건과 불일치한 서류가 제시된 경우 개설은행은 개설의뢰인과 하자 서류의 수리여부를 교섭할 수 있다.

③ 신용장에 서류의 지정 없이 조건만을 명시한 경우 그러한 조건은 없는 것으로 간주된다.

④ 은행이 선적서류가 신용장조건과 일치하는지 여부를 심사할 때 신용장통일규칙과 국제표준은행관행(ISBP)에 따라야 한다.

55 다음 중 해운동맹의 운영수단으로 성격이 다른 하나를 고르시오.

① Sailing Agreement

② Pooling Agreement

③ Fidelity Rebate System

④ Fighting Ship

56 관세법상 입국 또는 입항하는 운송수단의 물품을 다른 세관의 관할구역으로 운송하여 출국 또는 출항하는 운송수단으로 옮겨 싣는 것을 의미하는 용어로 옳은 것을 고르시오.

① 통관(通關)

② 환적(換積)

③ 복합환적(複合換積)

④ 복합운송(複合運送)

57 다음 중 수출입을 총괄하는 대외무역법의 성격에 대한 설명으로 적절하지 않은 것을 고르시오.

① 수출입공고상 상품분류방식은 HS방식을 따르고 있다.
② 통합공고는 대외무역법에 물품의 수출입요령을 정하고 있는 경우 이들 수출입요령을 통합한 공고이다.
③ 수출입공고는 우리나라 수출입품목을 관리하기 위한 기본공고체계이다.
④ 수출입공고, 통합공고, 전략물자수출입공고 등의 품목 관리는 대외무역법에서 규정하고 있다.

58 다음 중 해상운송에서 사용되는 할증운임으로 그 성격이 다른 하나를 고르시오.

① Heavy Cargo Surcharge
② Length Cargo Surcharge
③ Bulky Cargo Surcharge
④ Optional Surcharge

59 다음은 내국신용장과 구매확인서의 비교설명표이다. 옳지 않은 것을 모두 고르시오.

구 분	내국신용장	구매확인서
㉠ 관련 법규	대외무역법 시행령	무역금융 규정
㉡ 개설기관	외국환은행	외국환은행
㉢ 개설조건	제한 없이 발급	무역금융 융자한도 내에서 개설
㉣ 수출실적	공급업체의 수출실적 인정	공급업체의 수출실적 인정
㉤ 부가가치세	영세율 적용	영세율 미적용
㉥ 지급보증	개설은행이 지급보증	지급보증 없음

① ㉠, ㉡, ㉤
② ㉠, ㉢, ㉤
③ ㉡, ㉢, ㉤
④ ㉡, ㉣, ㉤

60 다음 서류상환인도(CAD) 방식에 대한 설명으로 옳게 짝지어진 것을 모두 고르시오.

> ㉠ 수입상이 자신 앞에 도착된 상품의 품질검사를 완료한 후에 구매여부를 결정할 수 있는 결제방식이다.
> ㉡ 선하증권상 수하인은 수입국 소재의 수출상의 지사나 대리인이며, 대금의 결제와 동시에 선하증권을 배서 양도하여 물품을 인도하게 된다.
> ㉢ 수출업자가 선적을 완료한 상태에서 수입업자가 수출국에 소재하는 자신의 해외지사 또는 대리인에게 지시하여 서류의 인수를 거절하게 되는 경우에는 수출업자는 곤란한 상황에 처하게 된다.
> ㉣ 수입자의 대리인을 수입국 소재 수입자의 거래은행으로 지정하는 경우 European D/P라고도 한다.

① ㉠, ㉡
② ㉡, ㉢
③ ㉡, ㉣
④ ㉢, ㉣

61 다음 중 선하증권의 법적 성질에 대한 설명으로 옳지 않은 것을 고르시오.

① 요인증권성 : 화물의 수령 또는 선적되었음을 전제로 발행한다.
② 요식증권성 : 상법 등에서 정한 기재사항을 증권에 기재 하여야 한다.
③ 문언증권성 : 선의의 B/L 소지인에게 운송인은 B/L 문언에 대하여 반증할 수 없다.
④ 지시증권성 : 화물에 대하여 B/L이 발행된 경우, 그 화물을 처분할 때에는 반드시 B/L로써 한다.

62 다음 항공화물운송에서 품목분류요율(CCR) 관련 할인 요금 적용대상 품목으로 옳지 않은 것을 고르시오.

① 서적
② 카탈로그
③ 정기간행물
④ 점자책 및 Talking books(calendar, price tag, poster도 적용 가능)

63 다음 선하증권(B/L)에 대한 설명으로 적절하지 않은 것을 고르시오.

① FOB 조건이나 CIF 조건처럼 본선상에 물품의 인도를 의무화하고 있는 거래에서는 선적 선하증권을 제시해야 한다.

② 적색 선하증권(Red B/L)은 선하증권과 보험증권을 결합한 증권으로 선사가 보험회사에 일괄보험으로 가입하게 된다.

③ FIATA 복합운송선하증권은 운송주선인이 운송인이나 운송인의 대리인으로 행동한다는 것이 운송서류에 나타나 있지 않아도 수리된다.

④ 최초의 운송인이 전구간에 대하여 책임을 지고 화주에게 발행해 주는 선하증권을 통선하증권(Through B/L)이라 한다.

64 다음 하역비부담 및 할증운임 조건에 대한 설명으로 틀린 것을 고르시오.

① Berth term은 정기선조건에 사용되어 liner term이라고도 하고 선적과 양륙비용을 선주가 부담한다.

② FIO는 선적과 양륙이 화주의 책임과 비용으로 이루어지는 조건이다.

③ Bulky cargo surcharge는 벌크화물에 대하여 할증 되는 운임이다.

④ Optional surcharge는 양륙지가 정해지지 않은 화물에 부가되는 할증운임이다.

65 다음 해상손해의 보상에 대한 설명으로 적절하지 않은 것을 고르시오.

① 공동의 해상항해와 관련된 재산을 보존할 목적으로 공동의 안전을 위하여 이례적인 희생이나 비용이 의도 적으로 지출된 때에 한하여 공동해손행위가 있다.

② 구조비(salvage charge)는 구조계약과 관계없이 해법상으로 회수할 수 있는 비용이라고 정의하고 있어 구조 계약과 관계없이 임의로 구조한 경우에 해당한다.

③ 손해방지비용(sue and labor expense)은 근본적으로 보험자를 위한 활동이라고 할 수 있기 때문에 손해방지 비용이 보험금액을 초과하는 경우에도 보험자가 보상한다.

④ 특별비용(particular charge)은 피보험목적물의 안전이나 보존을 위하여 피보험자에 의하여 지출된 비용으로서 공동해손비용과 손해방지비용은 제외된다.

66 미국의 신해운법(Shipping Act, 1984)상 특별히 인정되는 복합운송인을 고르시오.

① Carrier형 복합운송인

② CTO형 복합운송인

③ NVOCC형 복합운송인

④ 운송주선업자

67 다음 분쟁해결조항상 사용할 수 없는 분쟁해결방법을 고르시오.

Dispute Resolution. The Parties agree to attempt initially to solve all claims, disputes or controversies arising under, out of or in connection with this Agreement by conducting good faith negotiations. If the Parties are unable to settle the matter between themselves, the matter shall thereafter be resolved by alternative dispute resolution.

① Amicable Settlement

② Conciliation

③ Arbitration

④ Litigation

68 다음 국제복합운송경로에 대한 설명으로 옳은 것을 고르시오.

① ALB(American Land Bridge)는 극동아시아의 주요 항만에서부터 북미서안의 주요항만까지 해상운송하여 철도로 내륙운송 후 북미 동남부에서 다시 해상운송으로 유럽의 항만 또는 내륙까지 연결하는 복합운송 경로이다.

② MLB(Mini Land Bridge)는 극동아시아에서 캐나다 서안에 있는 항만까지 해상운송 후 캐나다 철도를 이용하여 몬트리올 또는 캐나다 동안까지 운송한 다음 다시 캐나다 동안의 항만에서 유럽의 각 항만으로 해상운송하는 복합운송경로이다.

③ MB(Micro Bridge)는 미국 서안에서 철도 등의 내륙 운송을 거쳐 동안 또는 멕시코만 항만까지 운송하는 해륙복합운송시스템이다.

④ SLB(Siberian Land Bridge)는 중국과 몽골을 거쳐 시베리아 철도를 이용하여 극동, 유럽 및 북미간의 수출입화물을 운송하는 복합운송경로이다.

69 다음 해상손해의 형태 중 성격이 다른 하나를 고르시오.

① 구조료

② 손해방지비용

③ 충돌손해배상책임

④ 특별비용

70 다음 중재제도에 관한 설명 중 옳지 않은 것을 고르시오.

① 중재계약은 계약자유의 원칙이 적용되는 사법상의 계약이라고 할 수 있다.

② 중재법정은 자치법정이라고 볼 수 있다.

③ 구제제도로서 중재판정취소의 소를 인정하고 있다.

④ 중재심문에는 증인을 출석시킬 수 있으며 선서도 시킬 수 있다.

71 제3자가 개입되지만 제3자는 당사자로 하여금 일치된 해결안에 도달하도록 도와주는 대체적 분쟁해결방법 (ADR)의 한 유형을 고르시오.

① 화해

② 알선

③ 조정

④ 중재

72 다음 조건부 청약(Conditional Offer) 중 성격이 다른 것을 고르시오.

① 예약불능청약(Offer without engagement)

② 통지없이 가격변동 조건부 청약(Offer subject to change without notice)

③ 시황변동조건부 청약(Offer subject to market fluctuation)

④ 승인부 청약(Offer on approval)

73 다음 중 분쟁의 해결방법에 대한 설명으로 부적절한 것을 고르시오.

① Amicable Settlement는 당사자 간 클레임을 해결하는 방법이다.

② 중재과정에서 Amicable Settlement에 이르는 경우도 있다.

③ 당사자 간 분쟁해결 방법으로 Mediation 또는 Conciliation도 고려해 볼 수 있다.

④ 중재는 서면에 의한 합의가 있어야 활용이 가능하다.

74 다음 대리점계약에서 대리인과 본인 즉, 당사자 관계에 대한 설명으로 적절하지 않은 것을 고르시오.

① 대리점계약은 계약에 합의된 수수료를 본점이 대리점에게 지급하지만, 본점이 직접 주문을 받았다면 수수료를 지급할 의무가 없다.

② 대리점계약상에 명시규정이 없는 한, 대리인은 본점을 위해 주문을 수취하였더라도 그 지출한 거래비용을 본점으로부터 청구할 수 없다.

③ 본점이 계약만료 전에 정당한 사유 없이 계약을 종료하였을 때, 자신이 이미 제공한 서비스 수수료는 배상청구할 수 있지만 이후 취득할 수수료 등 직접적인 손해발생액은 배상청구할 수 없다.

④ 대리점은 본점에게 회계보고의 의무를 지고, 대리점의 회계보고는 계약조건이나 본점의 요구에 따라 행하여야 한다.

75 다음 중 설명이 틀린 것을 고르시오.

① 한국 등 대륙법 국가에서 확정청약은 유효기간 내에 철회가 불가능하다.

② 영미법상 청약이 날인증서로 되어 있는 경우 철회가 불가능하다.

③ 영미법상 피청약자가 약인을 제공한 경우 철회가 불가능하다.

④ UCC상 청약의 유효기간이 3개월이 초과하는 경우에도 청약의 철회가 불가능할 수 있다.